Social Technologies: Creating Value Through Connections

S Darling

DEDICATION

To Barbara and Justicia.Jay, who changed my view on life, and inspired me to reach new heights.

S DARLING

This book is for everyone, because social technologies has made us all publishers.
We can publish, share and consume content on social media

Contents

ACKNOWLEDGMENTS

I would like to express my deepest appreciation to all the people who saw me through this book; to all those who provided support and offered me advice. This book would not have been possible without your support.

SOCIAL TECHNOLOGY

Introduction

Social Technology, ubiquitous, easily accessible to all, transparent yet a two edge sword, which carries both benefits and risks. Research shows that it delivers significant benefits to business and carries some risks, however, the benefits outweighs the risks and if the risks are carefully managed, it will be a very useful tool for business.

Today, as prospective consumers use more digital channels more than ever to research products, get company information, research prices, listen to word of mouth and recommendations from consumers like themselves before purchasing products, more and more businesses have realized that social technology or social media is a vital tool for their success. More than 70 percent of businesses operating around the world are now active on social media according to a survey by KPMG of more than 1,800 managers and 2,000 employees of organizations in ten major markets around the world.

Day by day the number of people using social media continue to grow. According to statista.com in 2011, there were 1.2 billion social media users. That increased to 2.34 billion in 2016 and it is estimated that there will be about 2.95 billion users around the globe by 2020, up from 2.34 billion in 2016. Furthermore, Facebook has over 1.94 billion monthly active users, Twitter also reported 317million worldwide monthly users in 2016. Over 2 billion internet users are using social networking and these figures are expected to grow as mobile usage and mobile social networks increasingly becomes popular. This is an incredible opportunity for businesses to gain access to a wider market to sell their products.

Social technology is a consumer focused tool. Businesses can communicate directly with their consumers and consumers can also communicate directly with businesses and with each other to share information. Businesses can

1

leverage this power to market their products to a wide audience on social media. Businesses can also collect unadulterated information about consumers as they interact with them and gain more insight about their behavior and preference and also use the data and feedback to innovate and improve their products and strategy. It is cost effective, because it is cheap to setup and reduces the cost of marketing to a large population as it allows wider access to consumers and relies on word of mouth to spread the message.

Before social technology, people were on the receiving end of a company's actions, but now, as more and more people use their computers and mobile devices to connect with friends, post their opinions and engage in conversations on social media, the tables have turned. Consumers now have more power and influence over businesses more than ever. They can influence a business positively or negatively by posting their opinions, sharing their experiences about a product or company with so many people instantly and at the same time. The very nature of social technology empowers them and facilitate their actions. It is immediate, transparent, public and highly accessible by many people. It is therefore important for businesses to understand the power of social technology so that they can use it for their benefit.

Although 70% of organizations worldwide are on social media, not all organizations see the potential of social media. Some organizations view social media sites like Facebook, Twitter, YouTube and Instagram as a networking site for teenagers with irrelevant content and are slow to adopt this important business tool. Companies that have realized the potential and invested early to harness the power of social media have reaped immense benefits, in some cases have had returns as high as 20 to 1, increased market share and are more likely to be market leaders. A video promotion of OMO (a liquid detergent) by Unilever on social media increase sales by 194 percent in just four weeks in Brazil. Meanwhile, those who are doubtful of this technology and afraid to take risk have seen their brand and reputation destroyed during disputes with customers.

Not only is social technology an important communication tool, but it also has the ability to transform the different functions of an organization including customer service, sales, marketing, recruitment, customer insight and IT, and its impact can be felt on the entire value chain.

Clearly, there is little time to waste as many of the world's most innovative organizations are leveraging social technology to create competitive advantages. Social technology is here to stay. Those that adapt and innovate quickly could gain significant competitive advantage. Unfortunately, those who do not adapt will find it difficult to survive the competition because competitors will quickly fill the gap and potentially, they could also see their brand and reputation damaged by dispute and critical comments that can go viral.

It is not enough to join social media and create a web page. Preparation, planning and a strategy are essential for success. It is also important that social technology is embedded in all business operations as it affects every functional area. Developing a robust social media strategy, which is align with the overall business goals with appropriate metrics and embedding it in all functional areas will ensure organizational success.

Businesses also face overcoming technical, IT, data, HR challenges and other risks in order to succeed. For example, to gain insight and a better understanding of consumer behavior, businesses will have to gather data (unstructured) about consumers as they interact with them. Integrating huge unstructured data with company structured data, understanding the context in which comments are made and extracting themes and sentiments can be challenging. Also integrating social technology to all business functions. IT security and loss of sensitive information is another challenge. HR is faced with providing guidance to employees as they interact with consumers on social media sites and also recruiting employees for new roles created by social technology. Businesses also face data protection issues, regulation and are concern with reduced productivity due to employee spending time on social media sites.

In future, as more tools and guidelines become available to businesses to help them overcome some of these challenges, more businesses will confidently join social media and will be able to leverage its power to deliver better products and services for consumers and also reap better rewards. Those that adapt and innovate quickly will gain significant competitive advantage.

Chapter 1

The rise of social media usage

Social media use worldwide is on a rise. The increase in penetration worldwide is partly driven by technology and worldwide usage of smartphones and mobile devices.

The number of users worldwide is projected to reach 2.95 billion by 2020 (statista.com), which is about a third of the entire world population. Majority of increase in users expected to come from China and India by 2020. North America has the highest penetration rate with 60 percent of the population with a social media account. The global average mobile network penetration rate is estimated to be about 34 percent. Facebook is the leading social networking site with 1.94 billion monthly active users worldwide. Global internet users spend about 109 minutes per day on social networks. Worldwide revenue from social media increase from 14.3 billion euros (2013) to 26.9 in 2016 and is projected to rise to 39 billion euros according to statista.com. So what is social media and why this continuous expanding trend?

What is social technology/social media or social network?

Social technology, social media or social network may be described as an application that enables people to interact socially and in the process create, enhance and exchange content. It enables mobile and web-based technologies to create interactive platforms where individuals and communities share, co-create, discuss and modify user-generated content. This includes all online and network-based tools, web 2.0 technology, systems and environments designed to enable collaboration, social interaction and information sharing among individuals or groups via the internet.

Social media allows people to form online communities where participants have access to content and the ability to create, add and change content. For example, through social networking sites like Facebook, people can form groups, interact with each other, chat, share, recommend items and give their opinion about a service or product. They can also add or delete content, endorse a product by voting or liking or disliking a content. Anyone within the group have access to the content and communication and can share the content.

Social media is not a new thing, people have been providing recommendations and opinions to friends and acquaintances for years through face-to-face discussions or telephone, letters and e-mails. Also, human beings have been networking in different ways for a long time. They have formed social affiliations and institutions such as public and private clubs, alumni, churches and lodges and have used communication tools such as the telephone, postal systems and telegraphs.

Social Media in the 16th Century - How Martin Luther theses went viral

In the 16th century, Tetzel, a Dominican friar was selling indulgence to raise money to fund Pope Leo X's reconstruction of St Peter's Basilica. He asked the people to use their money to fund the project to ensure their dead relatives were not stuck in purgatory. Tetzel's slogan was "As soon as the coin in the coffer rings, so the soul from purgatory springs".

Annoyed by the commercialization of the doctrine of indulgences by Johann Tetzel, Martin Luther nailed his "95 Theses on the Power and Efficacy of Indulgences" on the church door (then a notice board) in Wittenberg on October 31st 1517. His aim was to invite people to an open debate to discuss some of these issues.

Within few weeks, the printed editions of the theses in the form of pamphlets and broadsheets appeared simultaneously in Leipzig, Nuremberg and Basel, paid for by Luther's friends to whom he had sent copies. Luther's strategy was to pass the written pamphlet to a friendly printer without given them any money and then wait for the message to spread through the network of printing centres across Germany. His supporters discussed and recommended the pamphlets to their friends, booksellers promoted it, travelling merchants, traders and preachers carried copies to other towns. The printing press was a new form of media for Luther and his supporters to express their views and also spread the message. Luther was able to gain support for his views and also encouraged debate about current issues through the print.

Parallels can be drawn between the printing press and social media today.

Each technology significantly improved the way we communicate with each other. Through debate and discussions in both media, people are able to present their views and discuss issues. Each innovation also changed the way we acquire and disseminate knowledge. Knowledge was acquired and disseminated through the media and social connection. During Luther era, people read the different views through the back and forth exchanges between Luther and his opponents. Both media enabled messages to reach wider audiences and enabled people to read the views of others.

The printing press during Luther's era was a decentralised system like today's social media. Participants were responsible for distribution and deciding which messages to popularize through sharing and recommendation. A popular pamphlet would spread quickly without its author's involvement through the recommendations of friends.

As with "Likes" and retweets today, the number of reprints serves as an indicator of a given item's popularity. Luther's pamphlets were the most sought after printed material of that time, so many copies were sold. His first pamphlet written in German, the "Sermon on Indulgences and Grace", was reprinted 14 times in the year 1518 alone, in print runs of at least 1,000 copies each time.

As with direct communication with users, the printing press gave Luther and his opponent an opportunity to debate topics of interest. Tetzel, the indulgence-seller, was one of the first to respond to Luther in print, with his own collection of theses. Sylvester Mazzolini defended the pope against Luther in his "Dialogue Against The Presumptuous Theses of Martin Luther". Like social media, the audience had the opportunity to see both sides of the arguments.

Like today's social media, people were able to follow and discuss the back-and-forth exchanges of views, in which each author quoted his opponent's words in order to dispute them in the press.

Although the printing press played an important role in getting the message across to the public, many scholars argued that it was not the printing press itself which helped to quickly spread the message. This was because the printing press has been around since the 1450s and it had not enabled the spread of information in the same way as it did in Luther's era. Some scholars were of the view that it was a combination of the press and the wider system of media sharing along with social networks, what is today called "social media" which helped to spread the message faster.

So what is new today?

Modern social media is different from traditional social media by the scale, speed and the number of people we can interact with instantly.

Characteristics of modern social media

A number of characteristics distinguishes modern social media from other types of media.

Accessible: It is widely accessible at little or no cost. Anyone, anywhere can easily access social media at no cost anytime. Anyone can publish or access information easily on social network.

Usability: Social media is also very easy to use, no special skills or tools required.

Speed: It is instantaneous.

Scalability: It is highly scalable and instantaneous – available to and capable of reaching a large audience globally and operates in real time. It operates in a form of dialog and enables one-to-many or many-to-many social interaction.

Frequency: messages can be retweeted many times. Adverts can be displayed several times.

Permanency: Content can be altered instantaneously by comments or editing

Organization and structure: It is more decentralized. Participants are responsible for the distribution and collectively decide which messages to amplify through sharing and recommendation.

Transparency: It is public and transparent.

Historical evolution of social media

The evolution of social media can be traced back to the mainframe computer in the 1970s, followed by PC in the 1990s and the Internet. As technology began to change, scientists and engineers began to develop ways to create networks between computers which led to the birth of the Internet.   Their initial vision was to enable communication between computers.   PCs facilitated this dream as it enabled more computers to connect and to communicate with each other. It also enabled dramatic improvement in media production and storage and the Internet transformed media distribution capability by enabling the creation of web communities.

The success of computer networks and the birth of the internet enabled the exploration of institutional applications for social purpose i.e. U.S military's APANET (1970s). Early online services for social purpose in the 1970s included Usenet, Listserv and bulletin board services (BBS). Usenet and BBS allowed users to post articles or posts to newsgroups. These online services evolved to early online communities such as Theglobe.com (1995), Geocities (1994) and Tripod.com (1995).   The focus of these early communities were to bring people together to interact with each other through chat rooms, and to share personal information and ideas via personal webpages.   In the late 1990s however, the focus changed to user profiles, enabling users to compile a list of "friends" and search for other users with similar interests. Six Degrees.com launched in 1997 was one such communities that focus on profile. It allowed users to create profiles, list their Friends and, surf the Friends lists. Others included Classmates.com and Friendster. This was followed by Web 2.0 technologies, which evolved to facilitate user-generated, collaborative and shared Internet content. This led to the creation of social networking sites such as MySpace, Hi5, LinkedIn, Orkut, CyWorld, Twitter and Facebook. Facebook was launched in 2004 and has since become the largest social networking site in the world.

Facebook unlike many of the early social networking sites, like SixDegrees.com continue to flourish and add to its population. What sets it apart from other earlier social media, is its ability to innovate, trusted identity together with clearly defined networks, clear protocols, and exclusivity. Many early social media sites did not last long because users lost interest as the quality of their networks became adulterated with strangers and trust became an issue. Without trusted identity and a clear cut protocol for when to accept or reject a friend's request, friends' networks became full of strangers, spam, and junk.

Examples of social applications

Social networks: social media platforms which connect people and businesses through personal and business profiles to share information and ideas mostly based on 'Web 2.0" technology. Examples: Facebook, Twitter and LinkedIn.

Blogs/microblogs: social media sites which publish and discuss opinions and experiences. A blog is a regularly updated website that is focus on specific subject that allow individuals or small groups to discuss and publish their opinions and experiences.

Chats apps: are social media applications that enable individuals and groups to chat and share opinions online and on their devices. Examples include Line, WhatsApp and Viber

Social gaming: is a social media site that enables friends and strangers to connect to play games.

Discussion Forums: social media sites that enable people to discuss topics in open communities with access to expertise. People can share news and ideas. Examples include Digg and Reddit.

Media sharing networks: social media sites that enable users to share photos, videos, and other media. Examples includes Instagram, Snapchat and YouTube.

Consumer reviews/ratings sites: social media sites that enable people to find, review, rate and share information about businesses, brands and services. Examples include TripAdvisor and Yelp.

Social Commerce: a social media site that enables users to connect, engage in commerce and share opinions. For example buying and selling in groups. Example include Groupon.

Wikis: websites created collaboratively by a community of users that allow users to search, create, adapt and access stored knowledge and articles.

Shared work spaces: social media platforms that enable users to co-create content, coordinate joint projects and tasks.

Crowd sourcing: social media platforms that draw on the collective knowledge of users to provide solution to problems or input for tasks.

Why we use social media

The use of social media continues to expand. 79% of Internet users use social media platforms. Some studies have suggested that people use social media for different reasons. According to a survey by PEW (2016) in the US, the major reason why people use social media is to connect with family and friends. In 2016, 66% of online adults use social media to connect with friends and family, (14%) to connect with people with shared hobby or interest, 9% stated making new friends, (5%) reading comments by public figures and (3%) finding potential romantic partners. Networking with business contact and finding a job was another reason why people join social media (25% use LinkedIn (2016).

Another joint study by Nielsen and McKinsey also cited similar reasons including a desire to view and contribute to reviews of products and services. 68 percent of social media users go to social networking sites to read product reviews and over half use these sites to provide product feedback, both positive and negative and also learn about products. Other top reasons social media users engage in social networking include entertainment (67%), as a creative outlet (64%), to learn about products (58%), and to get coupons or promotions (54%).

Although this trend has impacted individuals and businesses positively, it has impacted other online activities such as searching, e-mailing and texting negatively. The use of E-mail has dropped significantly especially among users under 35. Businesses are using social media to communicate more with their customers. For example, Starbucks communicate with its customers on social media. Atos is another company that is using social media platforms to communicate internally with employees, collaborate with other partners and to drastically reduce the use of e-mail. The use of social media has impacted major search engines. More users are using social media search tools to search for information and content rather major search engines like google and yahoo. Consequently, traffic has increased from social media sites to websites like YouTube and other e-commerce sites. Before social media, people will first search on google for information and content.

CHAPTER 2

The Economics of The Internet

Market Demand

Market demand for goods and services online are influenced by availability of information, awareness and recommendations on the Internet.

The internet gives consumers the opportunity to get more information about products before they buy. iTunes, for example, makes it easy to sample music and consumers no longer have to base their decision on information provided by radio stations or retailers. Some companies have demonstrative videos of their products and how it operates on YouTube. Online users also have access to product reviews and recommendations which can guide and help them to make informed decision.

Consumers will only buy goods if they know it exists. Research shows that lack of awareness is a major factor in a buyer's choice and the demand for less popular products are affected because of lack of awareness. This represents a loss of sales as well as the reduction in the number of people who might buy less popular products if they were aware. In the music industry, as much as 40% of potential sales are lost because consumers are not aware of the products. Lack of awareness also affects the variety of products in the markets as investors will be attracted to products with mass-market appeal rather than less popular products. Therefore demand for popular goods are higher than less popular goods because of lack of awareness.

The transparency nature of the internet enables consumers to observe the decisions of other consumers. Consumers learn about products by observing the decisions of other consumers. Gartner reports that 74% of consumers rely on social networks to guide them in their decision to buy a product. A Vision critical study also noted that 72% found items by browsing a stranger's Pinterest board or stream, a friend's Pinterest board or stream, a retailer's Pinterest board or site, another social media website, e-mail or other sources.

Access to reputational systems on retail websites and online marketplaces also affect consumer demand especially for restaurant and hotels. Sixty-eight percent of respondents in a 2013 Nielsen survey said that they trusted online reviews. 78% of internet users consider consumer recommendations to be the most credible form of advertising. Traditionally, companies tightly control brand messaging and guided consumers through the purchase journey. The Internet and social media has changed the consumer journey. Consumer decisions are now driven by reviews, recommendations from global pool of friends, peers and influencers. This implies that demand for trusted goods and services will go up and demand for less trusted goods will fall.

Businesses can also connect and share information with other businesses in the same industry which will benefit them. In some industries and markets, especially in the semi-conductor markets where the market is volatile and difficult to predict demands, sharing information can be beneficial to companies. It can lead to better information and well-informed decisions. Sharing information can result in companies in the same market relying on similar information for decision making. For example, in good times when there are growth in the market, relying on similar information can cause companies to invest more in a particular market, produce more and make more profit. In bad times, when there are no prospects of growth, companies will invest less, produce less relying on similar information. Information sharing therefore helps companies to make better decisions. The negative aspect of sharing information is when the companies get their predictions wrong. This can lead to over-production, fall in prices and less profit because they are all relying on the same information. It's the consumer who gains from low prices when they get it wrong.

The Creation of New Markets

The internet has enabled the creation of new markets. A large number of new markets have emerged since the use of the Internet became widespread. New markets like Amazon.com, E-bay, Facebook, Twitter and Google have been created as a result of the internet. These markets have brought buyers and sellers together. According to a research by 8th Bridge, 99% of retailers have a Facebook page. Facebook has 1.94 billion monthly users (2017, statista.com). Google receives over a billion search every day and tries to match search results with sponsors. These internet-enabled platforms not only creates opportunities to match users with retailers, they also facilitate sales. A survey by vision critical indicates that 15 in 20

Facebook users visit the site every day, and 28% have purchased an item after searching for it online. The report further shows that that some social media users share prospective purchases as part of their active social media presence, in fact 43% of users have gone from social to sale. Furthermore, nearly 1 in 3 Facebook users have purchased something after sharing, liking or commenting on an item on Facebook. The Internet has therefore created a marketplace for buyers and sellers to come together to conduct their business.

Some remarkable economic features of the new markets include reduction in transaction cost, large scale operations, increased customization and rapid innovation.

Reduced Transaction Cost

The Internet has created the opportunity for businesses to operate in well-organized markets on large scale. For example, it is cost effective to operate markets with billions of users and with billions of products from around the world, because marketing and operational cost will be low.

The Internet also reduces some traditional cost related to organizing markets such as venue, staff and storage and other resources. It is cheaper and easier for users to visit online markets and search for trade opportunities. Lower search cost means that consumers can compare prices easily across stores. This results in retailers offering consumers competitive prices to attract more consumers. Research shows that online prices are on average 10 percent lower than offline prices as a result of transparency that search tools offer. The economic surplus gained by consumers in Britain was about £39 a month and $64 billion in the US in 2009. Lower search cost also increases retail competition. Distribution cost is lower online, particular for information goods. Furthermore, online retailers of digital goods can carry many more products and never worry about storage cost or about running out of stock, leading to higher sales and profit.

Communication cost is also reduced because it costs virtually nothing to communicate with mass numbers of people online. The Internet enables the formation of one to one, one-to- many, and many to many relationship, which facilitates communication. One users can communicate with many users instantly at virtually no cost. This reduces the cost of communication.

Furthermore, transaction cost is reduced because it is cheaper to personalize a user's experience. In traditional markets, it is expensive to personalize a user's experience, therefore all users are shown the same thing. On Internet platforms, a few lines of code can personalize a user's experience. Users can also be offered recommendations based on their preferences, past behavior or experiences of similar consumers.

The cost structure of operating on an internet platform is low, enabling firms to benefit from increasing returns. In Q1 2017, Facebook earned $8.03 billion in revenue. Average revenue per user (ARPU) for the rest of the world region was $1.27, up 40% in a year. Returns on online advertising is also high.

A platform can scale at relatively low cost to accommodate more billions of users. Many social media sites started with few users, but have scaled to accommodate more users. Facebook for example, has scaled at relative low cost to accommodate more users from 100 million in 2005 to more than 1.94 billion global monthly active users including about 1.74 billion mobile monthly active users. Facebook has not built new sites to accommodate the large number of users who join every day, it has rather improved its site and added more functionality. Cost of improving the site is relatively fixed, however, returns on investments to improve the efficiency of the site has brought scalable benefits.

Scalability

Internet platforms are intermediaries that bring billions of users together for economic and social activities. Many internet platforms operate at very large scale and are designed to scale at relatively low cost. For example, Facebook platform is scalable and designed to handle additional users at relatively low cost. Facebook employs less than one engineer for every million users.

From an economic perspective, businesses operating on internet platforms have the potential for economic growth because of relatively low operational cost, greater access to potential consumers, global exposure, and low distribution cost and consumer information. Companies are also able to effectively target customers using fine demographic and behavioural data to improve sales and productivity.

Research by (MGI) shows that companies using web technologies grew more than twice as fast as those with a minimal web presence. The Internet has also extended the reach of small businesses and transformed them into global companies.

Innovation

The internet has removed many barriers to innovation. Traditionally it was expensive to experiment and difficult to collect and collate user feedback. User feedback arrives too late and the quality was poor. The internet makes it relatively easier to experiment and test new ideas creating the possibility for relatively rapid innovation.

The Internet has not only removed these barriers, but it has also facilitated innovation by enabling access to immediate and unadulterated feedback. Organizations on social media can gain access to immediate feedback, conduct market research, collect information at no cost and use the feedback to innovate and offer consumers better products. Innovation is not only about the creation of new products and ideas, it is also about the refinement of services to meet the needs of consumers. Recently, when temperatures on Southern Rail trains (UK) became hot and unbearable, users took to twitter to express their anger, the rail company responded immediately by turning on the air conditions on the train. Traditionally, it would have taken longer to complain and response would come too late. Making quick adaptations and improvement to services have been possible because of quick and instant access to information and online feedback.

Another area of innovation is the use of codes to display different information to users. Using few lines of codes, organization can display different information and prices to different groups of users and also target different users with the information collected.

Customization

Customization facilitates a more efficient matching of users and opportunities.

It is often costly to personalize individual experiences in traditional markets, hence, traditional businesses use one-size-fits-all approach to offer goods and services to users. The Internet has offered retailers and businesses the ability to customize individual experiences as a result of low cost of displaying information and the ability to collect and utilize market data and match users' preference with opportunities. On the internet, users are shown search results tailored to specific queries, offered recommendations and offers based on past behavior or expressed preferences, or provided with information about the experiences of similar consumers. Businesses collect detailed data on user behavior and activity, which they analyzed to identify potentially successful matches. They also use the information to offer better services and products to consumers. This is what Internet firms like Pinterest and Amazon use to make recommendation to users. Facebook Friend finder is another application of this concept. Retailers can use the information collected to offer consumers personalized offers and coupons based on their preference and buying pattern. Consumers are more likely to buy products they preferred than what retailers may offer them and this will lead to increase sales and consequently more profit.

Advertisers can also target users based on demographics and online buying pattern. Unlike traditional advertising medium like television where all viewers see the same advert, the Internet enables online advertisers to target and match adverts to specific individuals based on their demographics or their past internet browsing behavior. An example of this, is Amazon recommendations based on browsing history or past purchases.

CHAPTER 3

The Impact of Social Technologies on Business Functions
Product Development

Social Media has transformed product development and innovation. Traditionally, product development was confined to R&D staff and companies use traditional methods of market research (i.e. focus groups, telephone and postal survey etc.) to get feedback during product development. Using social media platforms, companies can now tap into both their internal R&D staffs and a wider online community to solve product development issues enabling them to tackle greater challenges beyond their internal capabilities. Companies can gain access to additional resources and expertise to support them in areas where their knowledge and resources are limited.

Consequently, tapping into the knowledge and intelligence of the crowd in product development is becoming rapidly popular in a variety of industries. Over one-half of companies surveyed by Kalypso are using social media in product innovation to some extent. Crowdsourcing provides individuals with a platform to express their ideas, which are usually generated from their experience with actual product usage or observing others using the product. The ideas that come from the customer crowds can reveal rich information about customers' preferences and companies can tap into the ideas to produce better products. Companies can also capture value by co-creating products, gathering feedback and collaborating with external communities, particularly online users.

As the population of social media continue to grow, companies have realized the potential benefits not only in the numbers, but also in the wisdom of the crowd. Companies are seeing the need to more effectively apply the knowledge and experience of individuals, regardless of their background or vocation in the product development cycle to help drive higher levels of product innovation and profitability.

Those companies which have taken advantage of this opportunity by using social media for product innovation are gaining benefits such as better product ideas or requirements, faster time to market, faster product adoption, lower product costs, and lower product development costs. These improvements have resulted in higher market share and improved product revenue.

Early adopters of this approach like Dell, Apple, Ford, Adidas, Nokia and Starbucks have obtained a large number of unique, new and profitable ideas at relatively low costs from such initiatives. An example of such initiative is the Dell IdeaStorm. This initiative has enabled Dell and its customers to brainstorm, collaborate and share ideas. The project generated more than 12,000 ideas and implemented over 550 ideas.

Access to external knowledge through social technologies has reduced Product development time significantly. Ideas are generated quickly and tested immediately. Companies also receive real time feedback instead of the traditional way of using focus groups and survey, which entails organizing focus groups, sending out survey, collecting data and analyzing the data.

Furthermore, Social technologies have helped companies identify and address unmet needs by listening and analyzing customer data on social media. Companies can access the collective intelligence and engage all the stakeholders in the supply chain i.e. employees, customers, suppliers and other third parties in the product development process, exposing them to a wider range of ideas and real-time feedback. All stakeholders can contribute to the development of the product.

Next to generating ideas is conducting market research to see whether there is market for the idea or product. Conventional market research using focus groups is time consuming and expensive. Social media provides more detailed and timely information than traditional research methods. Generating insights by engaging directly with consumers on social platforms or by listening to what they say about products and features can cost as little as one-fifth as much as conventional research using focus groups or surveys. Consumer insights derived from analyzing data can be valuable input in the design and development of products. Social media can also be used to evaluate ideas before product development especially in engineering industry where mistakes can be costly. For example, Texas Instruments (TI) uses online panels to evaluate new semiconductor products in development. This enables them to identify products consumers don't want and avoid them in product development. Furthermore, social media can be used to hasten and improve the step of getting feedback on product prototypes in the development cycle.

Understanding the demographics of customers is another areas where companies are using social media in product development. Some companies are using social media to understand the demographics behind their customer segments in order to design goods that meet their needs. By analyzing demographic data and listening carefully to their customers on social media, firms are able to identify the needs of different segments of their customers and able to design goods and services that meet their customer's needs. For example, analyzing data like geographic location will enable companies to develop products using suitable material for that segment.

Companies are using social media to build traditional focus groups for testing products. They use input from social media users to test new products and concepts. Users can provide immediate feedback about new products and prototypes which can be used to improve products and services. One example is Kia use of input from social media to improve its Optima car seats. Just after the launch of Optima, the auto manufacturer learned from social media forum that the Optima was less spacious and uncomfortable. Kia was able to implement changes after a year using inputs from social media in less than the usual time it takes to improve design in the auto industry.

Some companies have created specialized communities to focus on a particular idea, Kraft created an online community of health and nutrition opinion leaders and consumers who struggled with weight loss to focus on its weight loss project. This community shared their experiences and developed ideas which Kraft used to improve its South Beach line diet foods. The community members also helped in other product development process like designing the package, testing and marketing the product.

Some companies are using pre-launch campaigns to educate consumers about the benefits of their products. They use videos and campaigns on social media to educate consumers about the benefits of their products and also to demonstrate how the products work. They also provide how-to tips and information about using their products on social media.

Companies are tapping into their customer experience in purchasing and using a new product. Social media enables companies to get customer feedback on the buying and post-sales experiences in real time and are able to immediately analyze, assess and correct potential issues immediately, before they become problems later. Consumers share their experience before and after sales and how they are using the product. Companies use their feedback to improve and refine the product. Project Sputnik, is an example of how Dell used post sales experience to identify problems and immediately correct them. Although developers have expressed their desire for a sleek Dell notebook PC with all the developing tools, the launch of Dell open-source notebook on XPS 13 platform did not excite them because the product was mistakenly priced higher than the windows notebook on XPS13. Within the first three to four hours of the product launch, Dell started receiving negative feedback about the product on social media. Dell was able to detect the problem by monitoring and analyzing brand metrics around the products in real time and was able to fix the problem within 24 hours. Apple also used post sales input after the launch of Apple iPad to improve features of the iPad. Post sales tweets immediately after the launched of Apple iPad provided insights for Apple to improve the iPad. By analyzing features of the iPad such as display screen with positive and negative sentiments, Apple was able to immediately identify problems, determine what users dislike about the iPad and use the feedback to improve the iPad and provide support in real time. The ability to monitor product launches in real time and fix issues in real time is very powerful. The traditional process takes several days and by the time the problem is identified and fixed a company would have missed out on lots of sales and its reputation on that particular product.

Examples of Companies Using Social Media for Product Development

Dell Computer Corporation uses social media to brain storm - IdeaStorm

Dell Computer Corporation is a leading electronic computer manufacturer and vendor with a mission to be the most successful computer company in the world. From a small computer start-up, established by Michael Bell in 1984, Dell has become a world technology leader. Dell aims to deliver the best customer experience by offering its customers the highest quality, leading technology, customize, competitive price and first class service and support. Dell sells desktop personal computers, notebook computers, network servers, and a variety of computer peripherals and software. It sells its equipment directly to consumers, mainly businesses and government agencies, by telephone and through its web site.

Dell redefined how computers were sold, by cutting middlemen and dealing directly with customers. The company's model focuses on engaging directly with its customers. It has for years used online tools to engage and seek ideas from customers, which has helped improve its computer hardware, software, services, and customer service. For example, prior to social media, Dell engaged directly with its customers online through Dell.com, Support.Dell.com and the Dell Community Forum.

Social media is a logical extension of Dell's direct model and plays an important role in its business operation. Dell has more than 21 million social connections through fans on Facebook, followers on Twitter, Dell community members, and more across the social web. This has enabled Dell to take its engagement with customers to another level allowing it to crowdsource ideas, listen, learn and engage with its customers while also sharing its goals of making technology work better for its customers, delivering competitive prices and the highest quality products.

Dell was one of the early adopters of the crowdsourcing concept with the launch of its IdeaStorm web site (www.ideastorm.com) in 2007. Ideastorm was initiated by the founder to get more ideas from Dell community. The company created IdeaStorm to communicate directly with its customers and to give them a voice and an avenue to have online brainstorming sessions, allowing the customers to share ideas and collaborate with one another and with Dell.

The goal of this initiative was to hear what new products or services Dell's customers would like to see Dell develop. Anybody could register and participate in the discussion. Once registered, an individual can then post any relevant idea. Dell assigns 500 Dell points to the contributor for each idea. Once an idea is posted, all the other individuals can vote on the idea. They can either promote the idea, which earns an additional ten points for the idea contributor, or demote the idea, which results in a ten point deduction. Individuals are also allowed to comment on ideas and to express their opinions in greater detail. Dell uses the peer voting and comments to assess the potential of contributed ideas.

Dell reports that this initiative has generated more than 12,000 ideas and nearly 550 ideas have been implemented. Dell also provides a monthly "Ideas in Action Update" to let its contributors know which ideas have been fully or partially implemented. Examples of ideas implemented include the Touchscreen Desktop and Blade workstation idea.

General Electric (GE) uses Twitter to improve strategic planning and product development.

General Electric (GE) is an American multinational conglomerate corporation founded in 1892, in New York and headquartered in Boston, Massachusetts.

GE traces its beginnings to Thomas A. Edison, who established Edison Electric Light Company in 1878. In 1892, a merger of Edison General Electric Company and Thomson-Houston Electric Company created General Electric Company. The company aims to solve problems for customers and find solutions that make things better for society, the environment and the economy.

GE's energy business is dispersed and complex, ranging from aircraft engines to water treatment systems, and serving a wide variety of customers. The challenge was over-reliance of its excellent in-house research and development capability and the need for fresh ideas from external organizations and innovative individuals. GE realized that to be a leader in the green energy sector it will need to integrate its existing energy resources with those outside the company to generate fresh ideas for innovation. In 2010, GE started an open innovation initiative called the Ecomagination Challenge, in which businesses, entrepreneurs, innovators and students competed for funding totaling $200m with ideas on improving the world's energy future. Further to this initiative, GE initiated the "social" airplane campaign to gain a deeper understanding of its customers and to generate more ideas using its Twitter account @ecomagination. Realizing the potential of social media to tap into the collective intelligence of the crowd, the company solicited the help of its community of more than 90,000 people who follow its @ecomagination Twitter account, offering prizes with Virgin Airlines for the best ideas. Conversations were organized around key topics using hashtags. In less than 3 hours the hashtags generated thousands of original ideas. The ideas generated centered on green topics, such as the use of solar panels and electric vehicles in engine-manufacturing operations and of LED lighting on aircraft. They also included ideas for improving direct communication with passengers when boarding the plane. GE used the insight and ideas to gain a better understanding of airline passengers' expectations and to create new processes for including stakeholders' ideas into strategic planning and product development.

Tesco Plc uses social media to create new products – the Orchard Project

Tesco Plc is a British multinational grocer and general merchandise. It is the third largest retailer in the world by profit and second-largest retailer in the world measured by revenue. Tesco was established in 1919 by Jack Cohen from a market stall in London's East End. Over the years Tesco has grown and currently operates in 12 countries around the world, employs over 530,000 people and serve tens of millions of customers every week. Tesco's core purpose is to serve its customers a little better every day and it is committed to providing the best shopping experience for its customers.

Central to Tesco's mission is the commitment to understand its customers, employees and communities and what matters to them and then innovating products and services that meet their needs. Tesco uses tools such as Clubcard data and social media to understand and gain insights to its customers' need and also engage them in the production process.

Social media enables a company to listen, engage and tap the collective intelligence of its customers, identifying new needs, co-create, test solutions to meet those needs and also gain acceptance before the new product gets to market. Consumers are more likely to accept or buy the product they co-create as they are involved in the production of the product. Tesco uses social media platforms such as Facebook and Twitter to engage its customers.

Asking customers what they want isn't new to Tesco, but doing it the digital way is. The digital way of soliciting ideas from customers is similar to Jack Cohen store tours in Hackney in the 1930s. He constantly travelled around the stores to ask questions, spark ideas, try new things. Digitally, Tesco uses online tools such as social media to solicit ideas from customers to improve its products and services.

One example of such initiative is The Orchard At Tesco program. This program was created to improve customer service, products and to "create a better Tesco". Members are asked to evaluate and provide feedback on the products and services that Tesco provides at no cost to the company.

Co-creation is a core strategy of The Orchard At Tesco programme. It allows customers to work in partnership with Tesco to create products and also involve them in decisions which impact them, from product ideation, range changes or store decisions. Tesco used the Orchard initiative to tap into the collective intelligence of the crowd to create the world's first community sourced wine. The supermarket invited its Facebook fans to choose the grapes, design label and decide a name for a new wine via an app on the social media site. Initially, members were asked to provide supplementary information of themselves, their families and eating habits to boost the data Tesco already hold through Clubcard. Members were then invited to take part in the project to either co-create, provide feedback and to start social engagement online.

Social media also helps companies harness additional resources and expertise to complement and boost their internal development capabilities, ultimately, reducing production cost and generating new ideas. Three judges, Tesco master of wine, Laura Jewell, Press Association's Sam Wylie-Harris and parenting author and blogger Becky Goddard-Hill partnered with Tesco in shortlisting the entrants to ten, with Facebook users voting on their favorite. The campaign also involved wine importer Enotria and PR agency Green Row. As part of the project, sales of the wine went towards providing a sustainable future for the families and workers of the Enaleni farm in South Africa, where the grapes come from.

Another Orchard project by Tesco is the sandwich project which was launched in September 2014. The aim of the programme was to give members of the Orchard At Tesco the opportunity to co-create a sandwich which would be made and sold in store. Members were asked to submit a picture and recipe of their favorite sandwich via social media #MyTescoSandwich or the Orchard website. Over 400 entries were submitted, which were reviewed by the Tesco Sandwich Category team and shortlisted to four finalists. The finalist were subjected to public vote by Facebook, Twitter and Google+. Over 7,000 votes were cast and Honey-Lime Chicken was voted the winner. The winner received a £100 Tesco gift card and the chance to see their sandwich being made.

Other use of social media for product development by Tesco include Tesco crowdsourcing a new flavour for its Tesco Finest ice cream range. Tesco used its Facebook page to canvass ideas for a new flavour. Customers submitted their ideas and voted for amaretto, cherry and almond as the winner from more than a thousand entries.

The company also use input from users to test product concepts or to bring in external ideas or solutions through crowd-sourcing. Members of the Orchard were asked to try the new product. After trying the product, members were rewarded with Orchard points if they write a Facebook post or tweet mentioning the item or write a customer review or blog post. Their input and feedback were used to refine the product.

Unilever used social media to launch an extra-mature variety of Marmite

Unilever is one of the world's leading suppliers of consumer goods with three main global divisions in foods, home care and personal care. The company employs 172,000 people and has a turnover of €48.4bn in 2014. Unilever aims to globally provide people with quality products which are good for them. With a vision to be innovative and to develop new ways of doing business that will double the size of the company while reducing their environmental impact, the company sees social media as an important tool that will help it to achieve its objective.

Harnessing the potential of social media will enable Unilever to communicate and engage directly with consumers to determine their unmet needs and to provide them with the products that they want. Consumers will be able to speak directly to the development and brand teams and have a voice early on in the development of products. Social media will also provide a platform for Unilever to listen to the views of consumers to determine what matters to them. Unilever will be able to involve users in product development process, gain insight through feedback to refine products and their environmental impact and ultimately to achieve its objective of providing people the world over with products that are good for them.

Research and Development is at the core of Unilever business operations and it spends about €1bn worldwide every year. Traditionally, Unilever uses feedback from consumers for market research, which is time consuming and expensive. Using social media has hasten and improved the steps of getting feedback on product prototypes for Unilever.

One example, is the Marmite campaign to develop a new extra-strong variant of Marmite, a yeast-extract breakfast spread in the UK, which has a very strong flavor and marketed as a product which you either 'Love' or 'Hate'. The campaign was created by the 'We Are Social' agency on behalf of Unilever.

Unilever involved consumers in the different stages of the product development process giving them shared ownership of the final product. Initially, the Ad agency identified and selected a set of customers 'super fans', termed 'The Marmarati' who were extremely active and passionate about the brand on social media and bloggers to work closely with the Marmite Research and marketing teams to help create the yeast spread. Participants were asked to upload content such as a film or poem or photograph on www.marmarati.org, and the best were rewarded and considered for membership.

During the trial stage, the 'super-fans' were blindfolded and asked to taste three different recipes for Marmite XO. They then provided feedback in person directly to the product development, design and marketing management team. The 200 lucky winners 'super-fans' were also involved in the final design of the prototype jar of Marmite XO and were asked to publish images of the two jar designs and get their fans to vote.

Winners were rewarded with a collectable jar of the prototype Marmite XO, as well as a 'taster' jar to sample, record and upload the special moments before opening the package. They were asked to provide their views on various aspects of the samples. The Feedback obtained from them about the prototype was used to refine the product.

Unilever involved super fans during and after the product launch. They provided samples to fans who were eager to get the product and engaged with them by answering questions about availability of the product on social media. Using customer feedback during and post sales experiences in real time enabled Unilever to assess and correct potential issues immediately before they became major problems.

Throughout the development process, the Marmarati continued to engage with the community on Facebook and Twitter, offering support, advice and promoting discussions about Marmite XO.

The Marmite XO campaign was successful launched and delivered in less time, at about 20% cost of a typical product launch. Social media hasten and improved the feedback process on product prototypes and the quality of feedback. The product sold out in many locations within days without an expensive advertising campaign and Unilever sold over £600K of the product in the first 6 months.

Nokia

Nokia uses social media to crowd source ideas – Nokia Beta Lab and Ideas Project

Nokia is a multinational communications company, a global leader in network infrastructure, location-based and advanced technologies with head office in Finland, about 57,000 employees and 1.3 bn customers in 160 countries. Nokia is divided into three major businesses, i.e. Nokia Networks, location intelligence business and Nokia Technologies, which is focused on technology development and intellectual property rights activities.

Nokia values based on respect, achievement and renewal reflect its way of working and responsibility towards its customers and other stakeholder. Fundamentally, its passion for innovation and renewal is a vital value for its survival in a volatile market. Operating in a volatile and constantly changing global market, Nokia is always looking at innovative ideas and new ways of working and engaging with customers to continuously develop new Nokia products and services. Research and development plays an important role in helping Nokia to overcome some of the challenges of a constantly changing global market, Nokia has therefore invested significantly in Research and Development. For example in 2013, it invested more than EUR 2.5 billion in 2013 in its 3 major businesses.

Nokia slogan is "connecting people". As a technology company, Nokia has developed many communication technology and products which has helped consumers to connect and communicate with each other, however, social media has enabled Nokia to take this to another level. Using social media Nokia can connect on a larger scale globally with all stakeholders and also fulfil its desire "to be present where the customers are". Social media can connect consumers together to discuss and share their opinion about Nokia's products. Nokia can also listen to their discussion to determine what they want and also gather feedback to refine and create innovative products.

Social media is an important tool for reaching people globally. Nokia has been implementing multiple technologies and online services since the early days of Web 2.0, to connect and collaborate with employees and consumers. Internal discussion forums and wikis for sharing expertise were amongst the first social media applications in Nokia. Externally, Nokia uses Facebook, Twitter and Flicker to engage and communicate with consumers. Tapping into the collective intelligence of consumers and employees through crowdsourcing, Nokia has created innovative products like the Nokia Lumia smart phone range.

Crowdsourcing ideas generated by users, Nokia has worked with consumers and other third parties to improve products. A good example of Nokia leveraging crowdsourcing for product development, is the Nokia Beta Labs, a social application that allows users around the world to download and try beta applications, software and service for free. The platform brings together developers and consumers for trials of applications, software, or services currently being developed by teams in Nokia or by selected third-party. Users provide feedback after trying the product straight to the development team via social media. They can write reviews or visit forums to share their improvement ideas with the app team and others. This provides an early opportunity to identify potential problems and alerts the developers before the product is manufactured. It also serves as a tool for giving feedback and interacting with users to hasten the production process. After users have tested the product and provided feedback, the software is either "graduated" to a final version or archived and removed from the beta lab's site. Customer feedback is an important part of Nokia's software-development process. Without knowledge of what consumers want in a product, it's very difficult to imagine what they want.

Another initiative is the Ideas Project. The Ideas Project is a community of more than 21,000 people, from more than 200 countries interested in mobile Internet-related ideas. The idea crowdsourcing platform "Ideasproject.com" was launched in 2011. Within nine months the site has generated over 7,500 ideas. It is based on open innovation and idea crowdsourcing principles, and it enables a two-way exchange of ideas between users and developers around innovation powered by Nokia. This platform bring together users including consumers, developers and other third parties to share ideas, collaborate and create applications for mobile platforms. Participants can generate their own ideas or comment on other ideas. They can work together with developers to solve challenges. One of the first challenges was the "Apps That Change the World". This challenge asked the community to share their ideas for ways to use mobile applications to make a positive change in the world. Ideas are generated through targeted idea competitions or challenges related to specific application categories. Users post their ideas on the Ideasproject.com and the community manager facilitates the creation process by engaging in dialogue, coaching and responding to user comments and posts. Members can comment and build on others' ideas and express their "likes". The best ideas are selected and pitched to the company and the winning idea is developed and distributed at the Nokia Ovi store. Through this social media platform, Nokia has enabled consumers to innovate their own products instead of the traditional manufacturer-led innovation. Users can develop products they want rather than what manufacturers think they want. Nokia also benefits by extracting external ideas from the community or by tapping into the "wisdom of the crowds" to improve products and strengthen the viability of its products on the market. This is a win-win situation for both consumers and Nokia.

CHAPTER 4

Social Care: Customer Service

Companies are now realizing the potential of leveraging social media to gain competitive advantage over their competitors and also to increase sales. Customers who engage with companies over social media spend an average of 30% more with those companies than other customers (Bain & Company). Today's highly connected customers expect immediate and consistent response from multi-channels. Companies who can provide additional customer support through social media as well as the traditional channels will gain competitive advantage over their competitors. They will be able to provide continuous support both online and offline and be able to engage and respond immediately to their customers' needs and also provide them with relevant experiences of other consumers through their social channels. Potential customers are more likely to trust the experiences of other consumers than the company, consequently, influencing their purchasing decision. A social channel can also act as another dedicated customer service channel, taking on some of the work usually performed on the phone by call centers. Companies will also be able to gain better understanding and insight into their customers' needs and behavior and design product and services that will meet their needs and give them competitive edge over their competitors.

Consumers use social media for customer service for several reasons, some of which include seeking an actual response from the company about service issue, praising a company for a great service, sharing information about their experience with a wider audience, venting frustration about a poor service experience and asking other users how to have better service experience.

It is important that companies get it right when they interact with consumers, because every interaction has the potential to go viral.

Companies can see it as an opportunity to build customer loyalty and a positive brand image. Customers who receive an immediate and effective response are three times more likely to recommend the brand to others. Users also share their experiences with a broad audience, both online and offline. According to American Express, people who have received customer service on social media tell an average of 42 people about their good experience and 53 people about bad experience.

Delivering excellent service creates passionate advocates who can promote the brand by word of mouth or on social channels. A research by American Express indicates that consumers who have used social media for their service are willing to pay a 21% premium at companies that provide great service. They also tell three times as many people about positive service experience compared to the general population. It is important that the user's experience is positive because it ultimately leads to loyalty, business growth and competitive advantage.

Companies can benefit from social customer service in many ways, for example, it can broaden the reach of the customer service department. By listening to different social channels i.e. Twitter and Facebook. Companies can collate and resolve a larger number of service enquiries that will otherwise be missed. Research also indicates that Thirty percent of social media users will rather receive customer service on social media than contact a company by phone. Companies that fail to take advantage of social customer service will miss out to their competitors.

Social customer service can be an opportunity for companies to improve customer satisfaction. Majority of complaints on social media are the result of poor service in traditional channels. Many companies fear negative social comments from dissatisfied customers, but they can actually use these opportunities to turn dissatisfied customers into loyal customers. An example of this is the exasperated tweets by Kevin Smith, Filmmaker about poor service on Southwest Airlines. Kevin Smith sent a series of tweets after he was kicked off a Southwest Airlines flight for being "too fat". Within a short time the tweets have been picked up by the Wall Street Journal, USA Today, ABC and other major outlets. The company used social media to apologize to Kevin and used this as an opportunity to improvement customer satisfaction.

Again, companies can use feedback from monitoring social channels to proactively identify problems before they escalate. For example, by monitoring social media in general, companies can discover problems that can be resolve immediately, before they become major issues and also provide advice even before an official complaint is made. Proactively dealing with issues can improve customer satisfaction and inspire brand loyalty. Furthermore, massive explosion of data from social media, GPS systems, organizational IQ, mobile phone usage and low cost of powerful computers and ever-improving algorithm will enable firms to anticipate problems in future before a complaints materializes. The concept of using customer feedback to improve production will be gradually automated through machine learning to improve the customer experience. This will enable firms to answer service request in real time.

Companies can improve Customer service through the use of social tools. They can post answers to questions about their products on social platforms. Customers with similar concerns can visit their website to find solutions to their problems. Those answers remain online and can be searched at any time (24/7), in addition, queries can be answered by brand enthusiasts and other consumers who are members of a community where a particular brand or category of product is discussed.

Furthermore, companies can gather business intelligence to improve Service Operations. Companies that combine traditional channels with social feedback will gain significant advantage over their competitors. They will deepen their understanding of the customer's journey and proactively recognize trends in sentiments around their products and services. These insight can be used to improve products and allocate resources across all service channels.

Increasingly, more customers are turning to social media to seek answers to their questions. A study of 23,200 consumers by J.D. Power shows that two-thirds of consumers interacted with companies for customer service, and only one-third for social marketing activities. Another study by NM Incite, a joint project by Nielsen and McKinsey, indicates that nearly half of all social media users have employed social media for customer service. Yet most companies are currently unable to respond effectively to the volume, broad range of questions, feedback, and complaints that customers submit through social channels.

Lack of resources and organization are some of the reasons stated for this situation. Many companies are not organized to provide social customer care. A survey by Deloitte found that only 33% of contact centers support social media. In many companies, responsibility for social customer service has been allocated instead to the Marketing or Corporate Communications, the earliest adopters of social customer service, who lack the resources and knowledge to handle the variety of customer service requests they come across. Another reason is lack of co-ordination between departments in dealing with queries from consumers. In some companies, customer service teams usually do not have access to social channels that are owned by other departments to deal promptly with queries.

To satisfy this increasing demand for social customer service, companies must provide immediate and consistent service across every social network. They must implement a strategy that aligns with their business goals and also implement a social platform that allows the different departments to work collaboratively to monitor and engage with customers on social channels.

How Companies Are Using Social Customer Service

Example of customer Service

HOW STARBUCKS USES SOCIAL MEDIA FOR CUSTOMER CARE

Starbucks a leading coffee retailer with 21,000 stores in more than 65 countries was first opened in Seattle, Washington on March 30, 1971 by three university of San Francisco students inspired to sell high-quality coffee beans and equipment. Currently, Starbucks product mix includes roasted and handcrafted high quality premium priced coffees, tea, a variety of fresh food items and other beverages.

It is one of the earliest adopters of social media for marketing and social commerce, and is currently a leader in leveraging social media for customer service. Their social media strategy is built around their company web site and 6 additional social platforms, including Twitter, Facebook, Pinterest, G+, Youtube, My Starbucks Ideas and ten guiding principles which include listening to customers, transparency, sharing timely information and personal attention. It is one of the most liked consumer brands on Facebook with a massive 37.32 million Facebook likes, 6.56 million Twitter followers, 2.98 million Instagram fans, 2.86 million Google+ followers, 160K Pinterest followers and 32K YouTube subscribers.

Starbucks is the most socially engaged company in the world. One key success factor is that Starbucks does not treat social media as a marketing channel but as a consumer-relationship building platform. Customer service and reputational management are of utmost importance to Starbucks. In 2008, in an attempt to improve its customer's experience it launched MyStarbucksIdea.com marking Starbucks' entry into social media. On their website, www.starbucks.com, they have a link "My Starbucks Idea" page. This page allows any Starbucks fan to give an idea on what could make their business even better. Mystarbucksidea also enables Starbucks to engage and interact with users. Users can generate and share ideas with Starbucks and vote on ideas offered by others. It generated over 70,000 ideas during its first year, many have been rolled out, including drinks and flavors food items, Order through apps, automatic ordering via swipe card, ordering kiosk, updated loyalty programs and splash sticks to prevent spills through the opening in coffee cup lids.

On their website, www.starbucks.com, they have a link to go to their "My

Starbucks Idea" page. This page allows any Starbucks fan to give an idea on what could make their business even better.

Starbucks listens to its customers. Facebook is another social media tool that Starbucks uses to engage directly with users. It is the fifth-largest brand on Facebook, with 34 million fans. Starbucks uses Facebook to listen to its customers. Consumers can share ideas, comment on ideas, give feedback, make complaints, and support request and product suggestions on Facebook. It uses comments and ideas to improve the products and services it offers to its consumers.

The FAQ (Frequent Asked Questions) page offers answers to many questions consumers are most likely to face. By posting answers to questions about their products on social platforms, Starbucks can address similar concerns for many customers simultaneously. Moreover, those answers remain online and can be found through Web searches by other customers. In addition, enquiries can be answered by brand enthusiasts and other consumers who are members of a community where a particular brand or category of product is discussed.

Unlike most companies, Starbucks uses Facebook to inform customers about new products, services and activities rather than selling products directly to them. Starbucks provides information that will benefit consumers such as nearest location, reloading cards, and job opportunities etc. that benefit the consumer more than the company. This provides value to its customers and help improve relationship with clients.

Through Twitter, Starbucks connects with each of the customers individually, answering their questions and retweeting some of their comments and feedback.

Twitter provides a platform for over 6.56 million Twitter followers to interact with the company. Starbucks uses Twitter to reach out and connect with users. The Starbucks team checks in several times a day and encourages dissatisfied customers to get in touch with the company for follow-up using a Twitter-specific email address. This approach ensures that problems are dealt with immediately before they get out of hand.

Most customers use Twitter to complain about products and services. Social media gives customers especially dissatisfied customers an opportunity to get their voices heard. Starbucks also uses Twitter to directly respond to queries, solve issues and to ensure that customers are satisfied. Most of the posts are responses to queries. By responding to customers directly and doing its best to fix problems, Starbucks shows that it cares about the people who buy its products. It also tweets product images and links to its loyalty scheme quite often on Twitter.

By also implementing ideas suggested by customers, Starbucks demonstrates to its social media fans that it not only listens to them, but it takes action. It also gives credit on its blog to the Twitter user that pitched the idea. The customers feel empowered when a platform is created for them to conveniently post their thoughts and ideas.

Starbucks uses YouTube to capture and share customer videos. Users feel empowered and they engage well with Starbucks because they see they care about them and involve them in their activities. Users can submit their video campaigns i.e. the sing-along love project fundraiser for aids relief. They also use Pinterest and Instagram to share their Starbucks moments.

Starbucks uses the different social media tools to reach new audiences, increase its visibility, engage with different segment groups and strengthen existing relationships. It sometimes post pictures of its products on Facebook, and shares them on Instagram, and pin them on Pinterest to engage with different consumer segments.

Starbucks believes in letting engagement and conversation occurs as naturally as possible. The company is listening, engaging, and making the changes that consumers want. It engages customers with campaigns and games, encouraging them to upload pictures in exchange for gift card.

By using social tools to build good relationship with consumers, reaching out to them, engaging with them and encouraging them to generate and share ideas, offering them value rather than advertising to them, Starbucks has been able to offer its customers excellent customer service and it has also built a reputable brand which customers can trust. For example it is able to respond immediately and deal directly with customers regarding their problems. This improves customer satisfaction. It provides information that will benefit customers. Starbucks' strategy is one where they will rather reach out and connect with each and every follower on a personal level rather than spam their audience with advertising messages. By also listening to them and implementing some of their ideas i.e. offer more discounts, bring back certain products etc. it is able to give its customers what they want resulting in good customer satisfaction.

How Tesco is using social tools for customer Service

Tesco Plc is a British multinational grocer and general merchandise. It is the third largest retailer in the world by profit and second-largest retailer in the world measured by revenue. Tesco was established in 1919 by Jack Cohen from a market stall in London's East End. Over the years Tesco has grown and currently operates in 12 countries around the world, employs over 530,000 people and serve tens of millions of customers every week. Tesco's core purpose is to serve its customers a little better every day and it is committed to providing the best shopping experience for its customers.

Tesco is at the forefront of new technology and communications, a leader in social media particularly social customer care. Tesco was awarded CCA's (the leading independent authority on customer strategies and operations) most effective use of Social Media Award 2013.

The company operates multiple contact centers across the UK connecting its knowledgeable staff with Tesco's customers. Some of the factors which have contributed to its social media success include its ability to engage with customers, offer them personalized service and local services. Tesco's ethos of 'no-one tries harder for our customers' is very important to the Customer Service team and has offered guidance to staff when dealing with customers on social media.

An early adopter of Social Customer Service in their business. Tesco uses social media to communicate with its customers. Their social media strategy is built around their company web site and additional social platforms, including Twitter, Facebook, Pinterest, G+ and Youtube. Using social media, Tesco is able to engage in real time to have a two way conversation with its customer. This enables Tesco to resolve issues and sometimes turn an initial negative experience into a positive one.

Tesco is committed to social customer care. The customer service team works beyond 9-5 office hours to respond to queries and resolve issues immediately.

Facebook

Tesco has 2.3M (2017) likes on its Facebook page. The company uses its Facebook page to provide online customer support and advice to their customers. Unlike many other retailers, who promote their products directly to customers on Facebook, Tesco uses Facebook to provide value to customers and only post one update each day, which is related to its brand or products. Tesco provides value and useful information on Facebook to its customers, for example, the 'Here to help' tab includes contact details for all its customer care channels and a 'real food' app that gives information on seasonal recipes. Tesco's post is aimed at educating and entertaining its followers. It also engages with its customers on Facebook by offering them incentives like clubcard points to share stories on various topics. Tesco encourages conversation among users by offering live chats with various food and health experts and initiating conversations that matter to its customers. The company also encourages conversation by posting food recipes and short video clips on their page. Consumers who have a positive experience with the brand are more likely to tell their friends about their experiences and recommend their products to friends and family making the brand easily recognizable both on-line and off-line and also increase customer loyalty. Some customers also use Facebook to complain about products. Tesco also uses the site to share brand news. A recent post informed followers that Tesco is now partnering with Diabetes UK and the British Heart Foundation. The Customer services team encourages customers to connect with them.

Twitter

Tesco is a socially devoted brand with over 509,663 Twitter followers (2017). The company understands the shifting paradigm of social care and knows that to succeed on social media, it must engage with its responsive and dynamic audience who expect immediate response to daily interaction. According to socialbakers.com, Tesco responded to about 7,128 questions during Q1 2013, answering questions in 8 minutes. This demonstrates Tesco's commitment to social customer care.

Its Twitter account is ideal for engaging and responding to complaints and queries regarding products and services. It also has a special customer care account for resolving customer queries and an offer account for providing coupons, discounts and clubcard offers on Twitter. Its knowledgeable staffs connect with customers daily on Twitter to provide excellent customer care and to resolve customer queries every hour. Tesco provides customer support daily beyond 9-5pm to widen its reach beyond normal working hours and to resolve issues on Twitter.

The Tesco care is committed to customer care and willing to resolve any problems customers may have. The customer service team does this proactively, letting their followers know each day when they can reach them, and even calling out to see if anyone needs help. Tesco also engages with its customers by offering them gifts, special offers and encourages them to participate in competition for prizes. These activities generate discussions on Twitter about Tesco's products and causes them to engage with the brand resulting in customer loyalty.

Pinterest

Compared to Facebook and Twitter, Pinterest is new to most retailers, however, Tesco is the most visible retailers on Pinterest. With over 43,834 total pins, 47,851 (2017) followers on Pinterest, Tesco has taken the lead with this tool to engage with its customers. According to Searchmetrics, Tesco's content is the most pinned material on Pinterest. Pinterest has often been associated with recipe sharing and Tesco has included this tool in its social media strategy to engage with its customers. The company engages with its followers by offering them recipes and encourages them to share the recipe. An example of this is the Tesco's Cranberry Camembert puffs recipe that was pinned 1,343 pins times on Pinterest. For Tesco, getting their recipes shared on Pinterest is a great way to engage with the consumers and potentially increase their exposure and drive sales of ingredients.

Tesco's Pinterest account has diverse boards ranging from groceries, inspiring home ideas, delicious recipes, healthy living, gardening ideas to helpful how-to guides. Tesco uses Pinterest to display its product range, majority of the pins links back to its e-commerce site. It also posts third-party content to gain greater exposure among Pinterest users. Part of Tesco's success on Pinterest is often attributed to the fact that it includes content from other sources and is not simply a vehicle for self-promotion.

Goggle+

Tesco has over 143,376 followers on Google+. Its Google+ page contains regular posts of promotional content, photos, how to ideas, charity events and news about the brand. Users share ideas, comment on post and Tesco also uses the platform to engage with them informing them about its activities. A recent post informs users of its fundraising activities and decision to donate to the Neighbourhood Food Collection. Followers of Tesco, occasionally use the Google+ page to air their grievances. Tesco also uses this platform to engage with users to help resolve issues.

Overall, Tesco is devoted to social customer care, and has shown its commitment to social customer care by engaging with its customers effectively on social media, providing timely and personalized response to queries and also providing out of hours care.

Resolving problems during first contact is also important to delivering positive customer experience. Tesco customer service team is equipped with complete knowledge on company products, deals and services in order to deal effectively with customers and queries.

CHAPTER 5

Operations And Distribution

Social technology is transforming business operations from within and outside its boundaries. It has enabled a new way of communicating, interacting and working with partners, and has also facilitated collaboration and knowledge sharing within the organization. Companies that have integrated social tools into their business have optimized their operations, boosted efficiency and performance, reduced costs and improved services. A McKinsey report on social technologies indicates that when fully implemented, social technologies give companies the opportunity to raise productivity of knowledge workers by 20 to 25%. An IDC report of 4,200 global executives also shows how organizations using social tools and technologies adapted at scale across networked enterprise, and integrated into the work processes of employees can boost financial performance and increase market share.

Business operation and distribution involve careful planning, organizing, coordinating, and controlling all the resources needed to produce a company's goods and services and to delivering the goods to the customer. The resources for production include people, equipment, technology, information and other resources needed in the production and delivering of goods and services. Embedding social technology in business processes will improve business operation through improving coordination of resources and facilitating collaboration.

In a large organization, each business function manages unique aspects of the business. All the units must work together to ensure success. This hinges on good communication, collaboration and co-ordination of resources. For example, the operations department must work with marketing to understand the exact needs of the different segments of customers. It can then design the exact products customers want and create the production processes to efficiently produce these products. The marketing department, on the other hand, must understand operations' capabilities, including the types and volume of products it can produce and the limitations of the production process. Without communication between marketing and operations, the company may produce products the customers don't want. This can result in poor sales and loss of revenue. Businesses can overcome these issues by embedding social technologies in their operations. Enterprise social networks can connect staff from different departments together, improve communication, and enable them to work together to co-ordinate resources. For example, Sharepoint, a social tool has improved communication between management and staff at Adidas Group.

Internal collaboration using social networking tools like IBM Connections, Microsoft Yammer can also improve operations by enabling employees scattered across teams and geographies to easily locate each other, locate existing information, share ideas and create innovative products. For example R&D and engineering teams in dispersed locations can connect together to share ideas or work together to solve problems. They will also be equipped with information and access to experts who would provide guidance and expert knowledge during production. Productivity will also be improved because the volume of e-mails and physical meetings will be reduced resulting in reduced communication cost and more focus on work that needs to be done.

Externally, Collaborating with stakeholders like suppliers, contractors and other partners will enable organizations to obtain real time visibility across the supply chain to meet changing customer needs. Organizations will also be able to tap into the wealth of information that exists throughout the supply chain ecosystem to enhance operations and be responsive to the needs of its customers. They will also benefit from increased speed of access to knowledge and external experts. In some situations, collaboration between competitors has led to the creation of innovative products (i.e. trash bag product), for example, collaboration between Procter & Gamble and Clorox led to the creation of the trash bag.

Optimizing Operations With Social Tools: Tasks And Processes

Leveraging and integrating social tools into business processes can improve operations through collaboration and efficient knowledge management. For example, manufacturers such as car manufacturers can integrate social tools into their business processes and through collaboration with their customers, designers, suppliers and captured knowledge within the organization, they can improve the design process. Customers can co-create products i.e. help design, configure and modify products leading to more customized products and better customer satisfaction. The time it takes to manufacture a car could be shorten and cost reduced. Growing competition and economic pressure has made speed and improved product development crucial to survival in the market place. Social technology can help address these problem through collaboration with customers and partners in the product design and creation process resulting in improved product and less production time. Effectively, social technologies can enhance coordination of business functions because of the connectivity it provides, especially for those using the supply chain resulting in efficient operation.

Companies will be able to collect and analyze huge operational and customer data for insight that could drive both efficiency and innovation to grow revenue. Based on the social media input, manufacturers will be able to analyze consumer sentiments and perceptions towards their products and services, customer service capabilities and complaint resolution processes. The insight gained could be used to improve processes and operations.

Social technologies provides better communication, which is crucial for relaying information about consumers to manufacturers across the supply chain. This results in better product information about customers' needs and improved production operations.

The development of the 'buy' buttons on social media platforms i.e. Facebook and Pinterest has transformed sales operations. It has improved sales operations because it allows companies to offer discount, target buyers and instantly allow them to buy from any location instead of the traditional sales channels.

Finally, social tools can be used to improve HR operations. HR processes such as pre-screening and recruitment of candidates can be done using candidates' profile on social media. Social media will enable HR to recruit from a large pool of candidates considering its total population and global reach. It can also help to effectively match candidates with required skills, ultimately helping to improve talent recruitment while reducing time and cost of this operation.

Using Social Tools To Improve Performance

Operational performance depends on quality, speed, reliability, cost and flexibility. For example, a company depends on its supply chain to deliver quality, the right products to its customers in a timely and cost-effective manner. In order to operate effectively, suppliers must deliver raw materials and product parts in time to meet production needs. They must also be flexible to respond to changing demands. If deliveries of production materials are late, or are of poor quality, production will be delayed, regardless of how efficient a company's operations process is. After production, a company relies on distributors and retailer to deliver the products to the customer. If products are not delivered on time, are damaged in the transportation process, or are poorly displayed at the retail location, sales will fall. In order to satisfy its customers and remain competitive a company must provide its customers' with quality goods, at the cheapest price, deliver them at the shortest possible time. Social tools can enhance performance by enabling organizations to improve the quality of goods, speed, reliability, flexibility and cost.

Increasingly, the ability to succeed centers on a range of knowledge flow both internally and externally to the enterprise. With respect to operational performance, social business offers value by enabling knowledge to flow within, out and into an organization. Social business can help improve operational performance by enhancing knowledge flows. For example, social tools can be used to instantly relay information about consumers to manufacturers across the supply chain leading to better product information.

Quality

Businesses want to satisfy their customers by providing them with quality goods, error-free goods and services which are 'fit for their purpose'. For firms that compete on quality, i.e. Marks & Spencer, embedding social tools into their operations will give them quality advantage over their competitors. Leveraging social tools in business operations will connect stakeholders like designers, manufacturers, customers, suppliers, researchers, NGOs together and enable them to collaborate on product planning, design and development. Businesses will gain access to experts, knowledge and intelligence, interest groups, and customer forums to develop quality products and services that will improve the customer experience. Consumers can also help design, customize and modify existing products leading to more customer satisfaction i.e. consumers can help fashion manufacturers improve design and production of clothes through co-creation and providing feedback. Businesses will also be able to connect fully with the entire business ecosystem in real time to identify customer needs and to provide them with a greater assortment of goods and services; early feedback from customers could also be used to improve products leading to better quality of products.

Improved processes can eliminate human interventions that could create unintended errors or delays. This can be a very important source of value creation especially in processes where even the slightest error have significant negative implications. Also, errors and anomalies can be easily spotted leading to the provision of quality goods and services.

The connected advantage of leveraging social tools, is access to data and information. Savvy companies could turn the data collected on social media into valuable information to provide meaningful and timely insights for strategic decision-making i.e. sourcing quality goods from the right source 'fit for their purpose'. Another example: data collected on listening to consumers and suppliers could be used to source quality products. Social media data could be analyzed to identify consumer sentiments, highlight issues and perception of products and the result used to improve services i.e. data collected on social media regarding a consumer product packaging was used to improve the packaging of the product. For example, analyzing consumer sentiments data on social media enabled a manufacturer to discover the difficulty consumers were facing in using their product i.e. opening a soda crystal container. The manufacturer packaged the product with a tight lid for safety reason, however, after listening to consumers on social media and analyzing the data, the manufacturer discovered that they had difficulty in opening the container, using feedback from social media the manufacturer improved the packaging leading to customer satisfaction and increased sales.

Speed

Fierce competition has made speed a crucial element in business operations. Businesses will want to do things fast, minimize the time between a customer asking for goods or services and the customer receiving them in full, thus increasing the availability of goods and services and giving a speed advantage. Connecting customers and partners together into operations process helps to address the issue of speed. Social technology facilitate responsiveness and enables businesses to respond immediately to market and product changes. Access to different suppliers, means flexibility for the organization, they can easily and quickly transfer to another supplier. This will enable them to manage volatile and unpredictable market conditions.

Again, real time visibility across the extended supply chains also enables better inventory and replenishment planning allowing faster delivery. A centralized order system also provides a single view of customer order, enabling better allocation and execution of orders resulting in reduced lead time. Better collaboration on enterprise social technology between customers and partners during the design, manufacturing and delivery process could also shorten the lead time. Managing procurement and logistics using Social technology, will allow instant communication between different parties on the complex supply chains and reduce lead time.

Speed is vital in digital marketing and sales. In today's digital world, customers expect immediate response to their queries. A research by McKinsey shows that 88 percent of customers are less likely to make a purchase if their queries are not answered within an hour. Social media enables companies to respond immediately to queries and also monitor their brands. Social technologies and analytic tools can enable a company to monitor its brands, products and also respond immediately. For example, by monitoring social media McDonald discovered that "#McDStories" intended for customers to tweet their positive experiences with the brand has been hijacked by some customers to post negative comments. McDonald quickly pulled the hashtag. Within an hour of pulling #McDStories, negative tweets about the company decreased from 1,600 per hour to a few dozen per hour.

Speed: Barclays Uses Social Media To Monitor New App

When Barclays bank launched its revolutionary money-sending app Pingit in 2012, by traditional means it was a success. But when it monitored social media sentiments it discovered that some dissatisfied customers have posted negative comments about the app. Through sentiments analysis it discovered that teenagers and their parents didn't like the app because it didn't give them access. Within a week, Barclays responded and changed the rules to allow 16-17 years access to the app. Social media provided instant feedback and in the process has shorten the time it takes to refine and improve a product for Barclays.

Flexibility

Flexibility is about responding to changes with regards to the production of goods and services. Companies can respond to external changes by producing new products and services (product/service flexibility) mix product, (mix flexibility), produce different quantities, volumes of products and services (volume flexibility) or produce products and services at different times (delivery flexibility).

Flexibility and adaptability is crucial to business especially in industries were demand fluctuates i.e. in the fashion industry where fluctuating demand can quickly turn profits to losses. Businesses will want to be able to change what they do, vary or adapt their operational activities to cope with unexpected circumstances or to give customers individual treatment. Being able to quickly change and fast enough to meet customer requirements gives a flexibility advantage.

Social technology could enable organizations to obtain real time visibility and collaboration across the supply chain to meet changing customer needs. Businesses could capitalize on the wealth of information that exist throughout the supply chain ecosystem to enhance operations in response to customers' changing needs. For example, businesses could capitalize and share information across the supply chain to improve distribution efficiency. This will enable them to offer consumers flexible shipping options i.e. premium fee, or lower cost options for free. Suppliers could also respond to localized variation in demand based on information shared on social networks.

Furthermore, demand sensing and sentiment analysis will generate earlier awareness of trends, either positive or negative for better preparedness and responsiveness. Companies will be able to produce new or mix products or increase the volume of production based on social data.

Dependability

Dependability is fundamental to business success. It means doing things on time, so that customers receive their goods or services when they are needed, or when they are promised. Over time, a business loses its credibility if it cannot deliver on time or as promised. Customers will turn to their competitors who can deliver on time.

Collaboration and better communication offered by social tools enables firms to deliver goods and services as promised. They can instantly communicate a customer order to their suppliers, internal staff and other partners leading to quicker processing of order. Managing procurement and logistics using Social platforms could reduce the lead time due to instant communication between different parties on the complex supply chains.

Also, real time visibility across the extended supply chains enables better inventory and replenishment planning allowing faster delivery. Real time visibility into all aspects of the manufacturing and distribution process will also enhance distribution.

Furthermore, using social tools and analytics, businesses can figure out which ports has the shortest "dwell time" for turning around shipments. A centralized order system also provides a single view of customer order, enabling better allocation and execution of orders resulting in reduced lead time. Better collaboration on social media between customers and partners during the design, manufacturing and delivery process could also shorten the lead time. Reduction in lead time means that customers can receive their goods and services when they are needed, ultimately leading to greater reliability, credibility and dependability.

Additionally, collaborative planning and scheduling with partners on social networks will provide customers with a wide range of delivery and return options, i.e. same day or within an hour delivery at premium rate leading to increase dependability.

Businesses can enhance their dependability using social tools. For example, listening to conversation on social media, they can detect early stock out and replenish stock or can advise customers on which branches have stock available on social media. For example, listening to an early tweet by a bargain hunter on Black Friday that a store has quickly sold out of the big flat-screen television advertised on sale enabled the retailer to advise customers on which locations have stock and to quickly replenish stock in stores which have run out of stock.

One core challenge for retailers is the ability to keep an eye on a product as it moves through the extended supply chains. With better connectivity enabled by social tools, companies will be able to track products as they move through the supply chain and be able to capture real-time status information. For example, companies will be able to capture real-time status information about international shipping and delivery. Dependability saves time and cost.

Cost

Low cost production of goods and services is a universally attractive goal for all companies because they want to keep their cost down. By doing things cheaply, organisations can reduce the cost of goods and services. Low cost production of goods and services will also allow organizations to reduce their prices in order to sell more or increase their profitability on existing volume levels. Every dollar saved on production is an additional dollar gain on profit. Some obvious ways in which organizations can reduce cost is to reduce the cost of inputs i.e. sourcing from cheaper sources and minimizing waste i.e. material, waste of staff time and under-utilization of facilities.

There are many ways in which social technology can help companies reduce cost, for example, by integrating social tools into their operations, organisations can reduce cost by scaling their operation. One of the challenges facing many companies is how to scale up or down as circumstances changes. Using social tools companies can efficiently scale their operations enabling them to reduce waste and stock out. Through connectivity and intelligence gathering enabled by social tools companies can have global access to suppliers, partners and employees making it possible for organisations to source products from a cheaper source, and also add suppliers, employees as when they need them consequently, reducing cost. Adding suppliers and employees when they need them, means that they will only pay for the resources they use.

Social tools can also help to eliminate uncertainties which adds additional cost. For example, many manufacturing organizations respond to uncertainty in order fluctuations by holding excess safety retailer's inventory stock which leads to increased logistics costs and inefficient use of resources. By collaborating, communicating and sharing information on social networks with suppliers and other partners, organizations can cut cost and minimize waste. For example, manufacturers will have access to their system and replenish inventory when it is needed.

Better connection between partners enables on-demand fulfilment resulting in reduced or even eliminating the need to invest in inventory before selling. In fact, many small retailers need not invest in inventory without guarantee of purchase, they buy inventory as it is sold.

Better connection and a single or centralized order management system makes it easier to spot errors and anomalies. Money could be saved in time and cost correcting errors and faulty products.

Better connection can also eliminate uncertainties caused by delayed deliveries. For example, retailers and their suppliers have insight into all aspects of their business transactions with real-time and status information and guidance, as well as alerts to problems or changes. It is also easier to negotiate with suppliers to ensure that they respond to delivery requests faster. This will also cut the value of inventories. Social tools can also offer retailers greater assortment of goods and services with unlimited "shelf space" at relatively low operational cost.

Additionally, Enterprise social networking interface within supply chain management connects all business partners and gives unmatched access to critical information which can be used to remove inefficiencies that add costs and reduce revenues.

Furthermore, real-time visibility, seamless collaboration and intelligence could improve operational cost. For example, visibility into inventory from order to final destination will improve operation, delays will be identified and corrected early and there will be no need for excess safety stock which adds cost. Internal and external collaboration will also improve operations between departments and stakeholders and help to minimize waste.

Using social media information, companies can analyze customer information to predict product demand. Traditionally, point-of-sale and historic data was used to replenish products and to forecast demand for products. The traditional method has limitations because it failed to capture real shopping experience, sentiments and could not accurately predict trends. Social data could become an additional source of information for sale and operations planning, using point-of-sale data and social data can improve the accuracy of sales forecast, detect sales lost to stock-outs, enable companies to effectively utilize their resources and offer better customer services resulting in significant cost savings.

Companies can also connect directly with customers to provide customer service in real time and at reduced costs.

Improved Service

Companies will be able to improve the customer's journey and improve services they provide to their customers. As mentioned earlier, companies can use social networking to connect directly with their customers to provide customer service in real time. This will enable them to resolve issues immediately.

Secondly, the ability to forecast sales more accurately using social data and other internal information could eliminate disruption to both manufacturing and distribution due to unexpected orders, changing trend and consumer behavior. Real time visibility and collaborating with partners could improve reliability and dependability, an important aspect of customer service. By doing things on time (i.e. delivery goods and services on time), a company can become dependable and a first choice for consumers.

Furthermore, using social tools to involve customers and partners in the core innovation process will enable companies to offer consumers improved and quality products and also better services. Retailers could also take advantage of the wealth of information that exists throughout their supply chain ecosystem to enhance all operations in response to changing customer needs, i.e. using social media in demand forecasting could improve the effectiveness of capacity planning. Intel, for example, includes social data in its demand forecasting system. Sharing, monitoring and tracking real-time data will allow problems to be detected early and solved quickly resulting in improved services.

Feedback and comments from social media could be used to improve products and services. Issues highlighted and insights gained could be used to improve services. Also, social media could enable customers to vote for their preferred product. This information could be used to predict demand to avoid stock shortages which lead to customer dissatisfaction. Walmart for example, uses social data and online vote to get a sense of demand for particular items i.e. toys and to plan early to ensure the season's hot toys are in stock and available to shoppers to avoid stock-out.

Burberry Uses Social Media To Transform Its Operations

Burberry Group Inc. is a British luxury fashion house, headquartered in London, England. It was founded by Thomas Burberry, a dressmaker's apprentice in 1856 with the goal to produce innovative, functional outerwear. The company designs, produces, sources and sells products under the Burberry brand. Product design and development are centered in Burberry's London headquarters. Fabrics and other materials are sourced from, and finished products manufactured at the company-owned factories in the UK, and through an external supplier network. Its main fashion house focuses on and distributes ready-to-wear outerwear, fashion accessories, fragrances, sunglasses, and cosmetics

Burberry products are sold globally through its stores and Burberry.com, as well as through third-party wholesale customers, both offline and online.

The company directly operates 497 stores: 215 mainline stores (brick & mortar) and 227 concessions inside department stores with flagship stores in key markets in London, Shanghai, LA and Paris.

Burberry's customers are central to the Company's activities. Burberry aims to be a leader in understanding, engaging and serving its customers, both online and offline. Social media plays an important role in achieving this goal. Burberry was one of the first companies to both recognize and capitalize on the importance of social media, first as a marketing tool and then in its operations. Over the years, their social channels have become key to their digital strategy, with major focus on Facebook, Twitter and Instagram. In 2016, Burberry was voted one of the 3 most followed luxury brands on Facebook and Twitter, and in the top 10 on Instagram. Facebook is Burberry's most popular account, with over 17,279,687 likes, and 16,865,860 followers, 10 million follower on Instagram, and 8.35 million followers on Twitter (2017).

As a global brand, Burberry faces challenges such as maintaining the integrity of the brand, consistency in product development, distribution and communicating and serving its consumers in a world that has been revolutionized by digital and technological innovations.

Social tools has helped Burberry to overcome some of these challenges and enabled it to transform its operations. For example, its marketing operation has been transformed through social media. It is able to engage with its global audience using social media with particular focus on targeting millennials (born between 1981 and 1996) to maintain the integrity of the brand. It also engages its target audience by communicating the Burberry story via social media campaigns with special emphasizes on its heritage and its innovative style and design that made it a leader in the luxury market.

Recent social media campaigns include the "kisses" campaign, a partnership with Google and partnership with mobile messaging platform WeChat at the Burberry 2014 women's fashion show.

Social technologies has also transformed research and has allowed direct feedback into the buying department. Burberry Chat on Salesforce's platform has enabled the company to collect feedback to improve its products. For example, the sales teams noted that large-framed male customers were dissatisfied with one of the retailer's suits. This information was passed quickly through Chatter to the design team, which made quick alterations to the product before production. Also, merchandising operations has been transformed through analyzing data collected on social media. Data collected on consumer behavior and trends was used to improve key merchandising functions i.e. by analyzing data on consumer habits, Burberry was able to improved merchandising functions such as which products to display where, which products to pair, deciding which products to sell in a particular store and which product are best aligned with customers' purchasing habits.

Communication and collaboration both internally and with external partners have been significantly improved due to social technologies. Furthermore, Burberry has been able to eliminate inconsistencies in products, a major challenge in product development across countries through the application of social technology. Designers and production staffs are able to collaborate across the globe to ensure consistency in design and production and also to improve productivity. Suppliers' collaboration, enabled through enterprise social platform also allows goods to be shipped directly from the retailer's suppliers to customers reducing the cost of inventory and creating an unlimited catalogue of products. Social tools has enabled Burberry to expand its product offerings at no additional inventory costs because the inventories are held by a third party.

Operational activities like customer services has also been enhanced through social media. Burberry offers 24/7 Customer support by twitter and live chat. This has freed associates time, making them more available to customers.

Burberry has realized the potential of social technology in simplifying the supply chain management system resulting in benefits such as decreased overhead costs, reduced wasted store and shelf space and other cost savings. It has enabled them to efficiently handle their sales operations i.e. minimizing stock-outs, improve deliveries through real-time data and collaborating with partners.

Promotion is another area that social media has transformed in the company. Burberry capitalized on the volume of its social reach to offer value to its followers. Fans on Facebook can see Burberry fashion shows before the celebrities who actually sit in front of the catwalk. Burberry has made the videos shoppable, enabling fans to click and order the garments on the spot. Burberry then collate the order and collects the money before sending the order to manufacturers in China and Europe. The order can be delivered at home or to a nearby store for collection. Burberry has saved lots of money through transforming its promotion and sales process and also eliminated product forecasting problem which is difficult especially for a taste-driven industry which changes fast. Traditionally, Burberry would forecast production for the following year with less accuracy, produce the garments abroad, ship them to its stores and other partners and if they don't sell it will then have to send the garments to outlet store to discount them. All these problems have been avoided by simply transforming the sales process using social technology. Burberry keeps less inventory and saves money by discounting less products and keeping less inventory.

Kraft: Using Social Media To Improve Research

Kraft Foods Group Inc., is an American manufacturing and processing conglomerate headquartered in the Chicago suburb of Northfield, Illinois. It merged with Heinz on July 2, 2015, to create the Kraft Heinz Company, the third-largest Food and Beverage Company in North America and the fifth-largest Food and Beverage Company in the world, with more than eight $1 billion brands, which includes iconic brands like *Kraft, Heinz, and Philadelphia.* A globally trusted producer of delicious foods, with revenue of 26.48 billion USD (2016), it aims to provide consumers with high quality, great taste and nutrition for all eating occasions at home, in restaurants or on the go.

Rising commodity prices, changing consumer trends and a traditional way of thinking has contributed to recent slowdown in sales. Kraft has been slow to respond to evolving tastes of customers, which are the result of a shrinking planet and the digital revolution.

Measures taken to address slowing sales, such as reducing manufacturing overheads and the marketing budget, have been insufficient. Leveraging social technology has transformed the situation and resulted in improved sales, for example, for Philadelphia cream cheese.

Philadelphia cream cheese has been around for more than a century. Leveraging social tools has transform Kraft research operations. Traditionally, researchers relied on small survey panels and focus groups. They had to visit consumers at home, look in their fridges, and ask them why they bought the product. Social media has allowed researchers to tap into spontaneous conversations on the Web, which delivers different insights into consumer behavior.

On one occasion, by analyzing consumer sentiments online and listening to conversations on social media, Kraft researchers realized that consumers were using Philadelphia cream for many different purposes including cooking. That was a big eye-opener for Kraft.

Kraft realised that they did not meet that area of need. With this knowledge, the international team of brand managers and research and development teams collaborated to innovate and expand Philly's target market. They succeeded in unveiling new product variations that have spread cream cheese far beyond the bagel to everyday cooking and snacking and also target 25-40 year old females that were more likely to organize a casual get together party. This doubled Philly's annual growth rate, to about 15 percent in just one year. Kraft's researchers and brand managers used social media and the Internet to share recipes using Philadelphia brand cream cheese. They created a series of recipe books and an advertising campaign that shows viewers new ways of using Philadelphia. Food Network star Paula Deen was recruited to talk about new ways Philadelphia Cream Cheese can be used. They also promoted this on cooking shows, websites, social media (Pinterest), and also used contest and celebrity endorsement. This attracted different types of consumers to the product i.e. those exploring, home cooking, healthy eating, and cost-effective recipes. Their websites hosted several recipes submitted by consumers. Kraft encouraged consumers to post their videos. Ten Philadelphia influencers were chosen to shoot an online video where they made their own cream cheese as the base of their dishes. Kraft convinced British retailers including Tesco to sell Philly next to main-dish staples such as salmon to inspire recipe ideas. Kraft campaign has been very successful. In the U.K. the share of customers using cream cheese as an ingredient almost doubled to 37% and sales went up 20% in Europe.

Social media has successfully transform Kraft's research operation, expanded the use of Philadelphia cream to its customer, enabled Kraft to track changing tastes, allowed direct communication and added a new level of interaction that acts as an excellent marketing tool.

Not only did social media successfully improved sales, it reduced the cost of research as researchers used social media data rather than visiting focus group at home, communication cost was also reduced due to direct communication with customers and other stakeholders i.e. focus groups. Collaboration with researchers also reduced cost and shorten the time to do research. Furthermore, the cost of promoting products was reduced as consumers posted their own content online as they experienced the brand and became advocates of the brand.

CHAPTER 6

Marketing And Sales

The most popular use of social technologies is in marketing and sales. According to a survey of 3,700 marketers (2015) by Social Media Examiner an overwhelming majority (96%) of companies indicated that they are participating in social media marketing. A significant 92% of marketers believe that social media is important for their business. That is up from 86% in 2013. More than half of the companies surveyed also said they use social technologies in sales. That increase isn't expected to slow down.

As companies continue to see the importance and potential of social media for marketing, more companies are exploring this tool and looking at ways in which they can leverage social media in this respect to their advantage. 38% of marketers plan to shift spend from traditional mass advertising to advertising on digital channels (Salesforce, 2015). Another survey by Regalix (2015) indicates that marketers intends to spend 54% of their spending on social media.

One of the reasons for the shift towards social media is the potential to influence the purchasing behavior on the consumer decision journey i.e. consideration, purchasing and loyalty. Businesses have realized that their actual and potential customers spend most of their time and interact with other consumers on social media platform. Their views and behavior have a huge impact on a brand's reputation and on a consumer's decision. For example, most consumers post their opinions about products and brands on their blog. Also, more consumers seek the opinions of others before making purchase, according to Mintel (2015), 7 in 10 Americans seek the opinions of others before buying a product. 72% of opinion-seekers age 25-34, look to social media contacts for recommendations when purchasing goods and services. Additionally, a satisfied customer is more likely to tell friends, families and others about the product and would prefer the brand over other brands when considering future purchase. A potential customer on a decision journey is more likely to trust customers who have used the product than the company.

Secondly, consumers purchasing decisions are influenced by the information they gather on social media. A study by Universal McCann indicated that 45% of consumers made a purchase decision based on the information they found through social media sites. 45 per cent of people who searched for information via social media sites engaged in word of mouth compared to 36 per cent who found information on a company or news site. Researchers believe social influence has a great impact on online sales. This is an opportunity for a marketer to help shape the opinions of consumers, influence the consumer decision journey and protect their reputation.

Market Research And Customer Insights.

In recent years, customer insight has been highly prized because organizations can profit from unique insight they discover about customers. However, to remain relevant and to gain a better understanding of the customer, organizations must change their approach to collating and analyzing data.

Traditionally, companies collate and analyze transactions and activity across the whole organization to gain a better understanding of their customers and their behavior. They use segmentation, historic data etc. to understand consumer behavior. In modern times, "knowing the customer" is no longer dependent on segmentation, statistical averages and historical inferences. This is because, the internet and social media has enabled individuals to interact with other individuals across the world. For organizations to remain relevant, they must collate and analyze additional information about their customers based on how they interact with the rest of the world and not just their organization.

Consumers are sharing information about themselves, their hobbies, likes, dislikes and what they value individually interacting with others. They are giving their opinions and recommending products and brands they have used and sharing their experiences with friends and families. Companies can use social technologies to gather data about their behavior and sentiments for market research. They can listen to their consumers on social media or create and participate in online forums to seek opinions about existing products and brand, and also present ideas for new products and get feedback. Insights gained by analyzing opinions about products and brands, competitor's information, new product ideas and perception of market segments on social media can be used to improve product development and design, advertising campaigns, sales, pricing, packaging and other marketing and product activities.

Companies can also test how well consumers will react to new products, pricing and other marketing elements on social media. For examples, in early 2010, Unilever launched a campaign on Facebook to distribute samples of its new Marmite Cereal Bar to test consumer reaction to its new product. The campaign was successful and Unilever delivered 33,000 samples of Marmite Cereal Bar in two weeks to its target audience. Feedback and comments left on Unilever's Facebook page such as "I'll be buying lots of those" was used to gauge demand for the product and consumer's reaction to the new product and packaging. Feedback from consumers was also used as input to improve the product.

Furthermore, insight derived from consumer behavior on social media can be used to improve marketing campaigns. For example, insight gained from analyzing the conversation on Unilever's Facebook Marmite campaign was used by Unilever to improve the Marmite campaign and also expand the campaign to Marmite 'Hate' Campaign.

Consumers are having conversation about products, brands and their interaction with companies. Organizations can monitor and analyze these conversations on social media to gain behavioural data, unadulterated feedback about their products, and consumer's perception of their brand.

In addition to monitoring consumer conversation, companies can participate in online communities, and also engage directly with consumers. Through online forums and community groups companies can ask for feedback about their products and marketing campaigns. By using online consumer panels instead of traditional focus groups, many companies have improved qualitative feedback, which was sometimes unreliable and difficult to collect using traditional method. Social technologies also allow companies to gain access to a wider sampling size compared to traditional focus groups. Inputs from a wider sampling size is more efficient in improving market research outcome.

Companies can gain more knowledge of their consumer behavior and how they perceive and use their products by tracking conversation on social media platforms. For example, by listening to online conversation, Kraft learned that consumers were using Philadelphia Cream not only as spread for their bagel and cheesecake ingredient but for other purposes i.e. dips and sauces. Insight gained from listening to consumer conversation was used as input to create 'how-to' videos to reiterate the different use of the products and to target new users.

Effective campaign requires that companies test their campaigns to see whether consumers will respond favorably before implementing the actual campaign, otherwise lots of money and time could be wasted on unsuccessful campaigns. Social media provides access to a wider selection of consumers, which companies can target their test adverts at and get instant feedback on their campaigns. Unadulterated feedback and insight gained can be used to improve advertising campaign.

Social technologies offers a more efficient way of segmenting consumers than the traditional media. It provides more detailed profile and behavior data. For example in addition to demographic details of consumers such as age, sex, post code, companies have access to extra information like hobbies, color preference, interest etc. Furthermore, social media profiles contain a wealth of demographic information and behavioural footprints that are, in most cases, much more personal and of remarkably high quality because invalid information is difficult to maintain in a network of friends who can challenge false claims. Companies therefore have access to breadth and quality of data that will be impossible to access using traditional methods, which can provide an effective segmentation to target potential clients.

Companies can also monitor social conversation to track competitors' moves. They can use the insights gained from monitoring conversation to adjust or phase their own marketing campaigns.

Marketing Communication

Social media has magnified communication between consumers and businesses. It has enabled one person to communicate with thousands of other people about products and brands and also companies to communicate with consumers. Companies can talk to customers through social media platforms like Facebook, Twitter and blogs.

In a sense, the role of social media in enabling customers to talk to one another is an extension of traditional word-of-mouth communication. Consumers can use social media to tell their friends and family about a good or bad experience with a product. Traditionally, a dissatisfied customer can only tell a few people about their experience, but with social media they can tell thousands of people with a few key strokes. An example of a bad experience is the story of Vincent Ferrari. Vincent, a blogger, posted an audio recording of his bad experience with AOL customer service representatives which went "viral" and was picked up by the main stream media and other bloggers and websites. In the same way, a good experience could go viral and improve the reputation of a company or promote its products. The challenge for companies is how to harness this power for their benefit.

Social media provides a platform for companies to communicate directly with consumers at less cost and with greater reach than traditional method. For example, a few years ago, manufacturers had limited contact with consumers because their products were sold through retailers. Social technologies has now made it possible for manufacturers to communicate and engage directly with their consumers. A typical example of this is the "Dove campaign for real beauty". Unilever used social media platform to communicate their values and to engage consumers on issues that affect them.

Social technologies can be used to provide information about products and brands. Traditionally, companies use brochures and sales representatives to provide information about the benefits of a product. By contrast, social technologies have enabled companies to provide information about products and services on social media or direct potential consumers to their website. Furthermore, companies can get real-time feedback from consumers, competitors and experts through online discussions on social media. Some companies, e.g. Johnson & Johnsons have also created online educational videos to share on social media platform site like YouTube to educate consumers of the benefits of their products or any potential health issues and concerns.

The ability to communicate instantly, in real-time and utilize multi-media formats like Facebook, Twitter and YouTube makes social media an effective promotional tool to reach people globally. Ford Motor Company used social media to promote the release of its new model Ford Focus. The company selected 40 Social Media users and gave them each a Focus to test at a test track in Spain which was videoed. The videos were then distributed via Facebook, Twitter, and other social media platforms.

Additionally, companies can use social technologies like Twitter and Facebook to inform consumers about new products, product success and promotional products and discounts. Not only can retailers use social media as a promotional tool, they can co-operate with consumers to co-create marketing campaigns and provide content. Doritos, for example, launched an online competition in which consumers submitted videos for the snack brand Super Bowl campaign. Contestants could submit, watch and vote for the videos online and Doritos broadcast the winner during the Super Bowl. More than 6,100 videos were submitted and the winning videos was voted the number one video in the USA Today's/Facebook Super Bowl. .

Social Commerce

Another application of social technologies in marketing & sales is in social commerce. The last few decades have seen major transformation in the way we shop, from brick and mortar, to e-commerce and then to social commerce. Social commerce is the integration of electronic commerce and social media to assist online buying and selling of products and services.

Unlike many new technologies to emerge over the years, social commerce has had a rapid adoption. Great strides have also been made to make social media easy and convenient for the benefit of both the retailer and the consumer. Features of social commerce include user ratings, referrals, reviews and recommendations, online and social advertising. Shoppers rely on reviews and recommendations of their social connection and community to assist them in shopping online. Basically, social commerce is the use of social network in the context of e-commerce transactions.

Social networks are becoming the new online market place as the population of social media and online shoppers continue to grow. An overwhelming majority of people surveyed by Social Media Examiner (2015) indicated that they are participating in social media marketing. Also, more shoppers are looking to Facebook, Twitter, Instagram and other social media sites for their next online purchase. Another research by loyalty analytic shows that one-third (33%) of 18- to 24-year-olds would like to purchase items directly from Facebook as they leverage online reviews, comments and recommendations.

Reviews and recommendation shared with online contact spreads faster than traditional word-of-mouth or advert. Social technology has therefore expanded traditional word-of-mouth as consumers seek advice from social connection online before purchasing products. Social commerce may also be described as the application of word-of-mouth to e-commerce.

The surge in social commerce may be due to customers looking for ways to leverage each other's expertise, the desire to understand what they are purchasing, and make more informed and accurate purchase decisions.

This trend towards social commerce has caused many retailer and social networks to partner to offer consumers a more convenient online shopping experience. Social networks working in partnership with retailers have introduced the "buy" button to enable brands to sell directly via social media instead of being redirected to the retailer's website. For example, in 2015, we saw major developments including the introduction of the new buy button by Twitter, Facebook, and YouTube to make their sites and apps more e-commerce-friendly, Pinterest's launched the "Buy it" button and Instagram's expanded its ad program. Instagram new direct response ad format allows users to take action on posts through buttons such as 'shop now', 'install' or 'learn more'.

Benefits To Consumers

Social commerce is advantageous to both consumers and retailers. For example, consumers get access to trustworthy people in their online social community who have used the product and are therefore able to seek advice from them before buying a product.

Consumers understand what they are buying from more detailed product description, reviews, comments and information on how the products work, how-to tips and videos and are able to make more informed and accurate purchase decisions.

Furthermore, consumers are able to measure the value they get for their money through information shared on social media.

Benefits To Retailers

Retailers also benefit by adding social commerce features to their sites. For example , by creating communities where the discussions centers around their brand, product, and lifestyle businesses can create a lively and more effective online experience leading to return visits and consequently increased sales.

Secondly, retailers benefit from increased brand loyalty as a result of consumers seeking each other expertise and advice about product use and benefit in online community. Research shows that consumer ratings, reviews and comments significantly affect sales of online books and digital products. Furthermore, studies show that active consumers in the community are more likely to generate about ten times the revenue of an average consumer. Active engagement with user communities improves the bond between consumers and the brand and potentially increases sales.

Integrating social technology into the core experience of a retail website enables shoppers to interact with product, brand, and life-style related content resulting in increased preference for the brand and ultimately increased sales.

Additionally, retailers benefit from larger and more engaged audiences and increased conversion rates leading to increased revenue and profitability from their online channels.

Content relevant to products and lifestyles can drive new traffic to the site. For example, a retailer who publishes a how-to article or video about its products would attract users searching for information or instructions on how to use the product or fix issue relating to the product. Highly qualified new site visitors who are eager to solve problems are more likely to buy products or services to solve problems. Furthermore, social commerce can drive these new, engaged visitors to complete sales. Potential customers are able to discuss product benefits, features and application with members of their social community, who influence them in the purchase process.

Retailers have access to consumer feedback by listening to conversation and engaging with consumers. A high number of negative customer rating about a product is an indication that the product is performing below expectation or faulty. Gaining visibility into these issues early on, retailers can reduce return rates and improve customer satisfaction dramatically.

Social commerce offers a real opportunity for retailers to shorten the path to purchase. The introduction of the 'buy button', 'shop now' or other action button has enabled direct purchasing from consumers and given retailers an opportunity to sell directly to consumers. Prior to that, consumer where directed to the retailer's website, but with the introduction of the 'buy button' Facebook users can buy items on the platform instead of being directed to a retailer's website. Instagram users can also take action on posts by clicking 'shop now', 'install' or 'learn more'.

Finally, retailers can easily analyze purchase patterns by connecting purchase pattern with consumers' detailed demographics. This enables retailers to make more informed decision i.e. targeting new customers with offers and discounts and offering existing customers better deals. Digital distribution of offers and discounts reduces coupon redemption time and lowers lower distribution costs.

Social Commerce: Challenges

Despite the potential benefits of social commerce, retailers face many challenges in social marketing. Some of the challenges they face include the risk of negative comments which might affect sales, secure payment system and competition from social network providers.

Research shows a correlation between revenue and rating and review. Retailers have observed an increase in revenue when users are allowed to post ratings and reviews, however, there is the risk that users will post negative comments about products, which can have a devastating effect on sales and consequently profit. Retailers can overcome this challenge by continuously monitoring social media for their brand and products and responding immediately to negative comments if necessary and also engaging with customers to increase trust.

Secondly, retailers face the challenge of providing a convenient and secure payments system to facilitate payment online. A convenient, reliable and secure payment system is essential for success in social commerce. Great strides have been made in providing payment systems online, for example, social technology providers like Facebook or traditional payment players like banks and credit card companies are providing users with convenient payment systems. Examples of such system are Snapcash, Vemo, Google Wallet, Apple Pay and Twitter Buy. Currently, there are two major categories of social payment, they are peer-to-peer transfers (Snapcash) and online purchases (Apple Pay).

It is difficult to predict how this business model will evolve in the social technology age. Some major social networks are looking to cut out the middle man, and to introduce payment methods directly on the channel's sponsored messaging. Many companies are also seeking partnership with major networks and digital currency firms. For example, Barclays has become the first big British bank to form a partnership with a digital currency firm, social payments app Circle. Whatever direction the evolution of the social payment system takes, it is important that networks and companies work together to protect consumer data and improve security online.

Finally, retailers may face competition from network providers. Social platform providers could either sell goods themselves or allow others to use their platform to facilitate third party sales for commission.

Lead Generation

One of the biggest challenges facing marketers today is generating quality leads. In a study (2013) by IDG, 61% of marketers reported that generating high quality leads was a big problem for their organization. Lack of resources such as staff, budget and time were named as some of the barriers to generating quality leads. Social media plays an important role in helping marketers overcome these barriers. With less resources retailers can generate quality leads. For example, Social marketers (2015) reported that, for as little as 6 hours a week, more than 66% of marketers saw lead generation benefits with social media and more than half of marketers surveyed saw a benefit of reduced marketing expenses. Another example, is the reduction of ad budget by Procter & Gamble (P&G). Ad budget took a lion share of P&G's ad budget, but with social media it generated more leads than the traditional media.

With the wealth of information available on the internet and social media, potential buyers research companies and products before they make any purchase commitment. Often, retailers offer more information about product features than about how the product truly solve the customer's problem. One effective way to make a strong impression on potential buyers in their early search is to provide them with an authentic and insightful content that meet their needs i.e. cost reduction, reliability etc. Social media is a useful platforms for distributing these type of content to keep customers engaged and generating sales leads. For example, Dell used Twitter to alert its potential buyers to exclusive deals which met the needs of customers looking for quality product at lower prices. This generated quality leads and led to increase sales and revenue.

A lead is the contact information and in some cases, demographic information of a customer who is interested in a specific product or service. Potential customers interested in the company's products may provide information such as name and e-mail address in exchange for discount or vouchers. These are basic information that will enable the company to communicate with the to-be lead. Organisations use the information collected to initiate communication and personalize offers to meet their customers' needs.

To provide products that effectively meet the needs of the customers, retailers must understand their needs. Social media is an effective tool for that, because it enables retailers to gather accurate, precise and timely information about prospective contacts in the marketplace. By joining and participating in social networking sites, sales staff can gain access, view and collect information about prospective buyers and generate leads. Prospective buyers can also view information about the company.

Furthermore, a company can generate future client list by allowing open membership on its product blog. Precise and accurate information gathered by companies through open membership can be used to generate leads and to gain business opportunities. For example, many companies actively participate on social media including LinkedIn, Twitter and Facebook to find talent or market their new products and services.

Leads generation includes activities that could spark interest in a product, for example viewing a YouTube video about a product. A SellPoint study conducted by Coremetrics8 found that users were more likely to buy products after viewing video tours. The study tested over 1 million shoppers' behaviour on the CompUSA website over a 60-day period. Also, potential buyers looking to purchase a particular product, are more likely turn to social media to read reviews and comments from their peers before they take the plunge. A good review or comment online generates lead and can influence a potential buyer.

Improve Sales

It takes time to build trust and develop relationships that lead to sales. However, a large percentage of marketers who persist find great results. According to Social Media Marketing (2015) more than half of marketers who've been using social media for at least 2 years reported that, it helped them improve sales. 73% of those who spend 40+ hours per week earn new business through their efforts.

Social technology can be a useful post sales and follow up tool. The ability to communicate and interact with the customers enables customers to post any issues relating to products and allows the retailer to address the issue on social media. Retailers can add online forms for customers to initiate service requests. Companies can also interact or share information with customers to remain proactive on customer service needs. Additionally, retailers can use social media to ask for referrals for future sales and cross-sell other products. Furthermore, retailers can use social media to communicate success stories i.e. via Twitter. Customers can also post testimonies about their experience.

CHAPTER 7

Business Support

Business support is part of administrative activities which includes IT, HR, Marketing, Project Management or Training. Communication and Collaboration are essential to the success of business support functions. Social tools are effective tools for enhancing communication and collaboration.

Collaboration And Communication

As stated previously, most organizations particularly large organizations are divided into smaller groups by area of specialty (functional departments) such as sales, IT, finance, marketing etc. Functional departments creates greater efficiency because of specialization, however, isolation and poor communication between the various departments may potentially decrease flexibility, growth and innovation. To grow, innovate and gain competitive advantage in today's dynamic world, businesses must rapidly create value, accelerate innovation and increase operational efficiency. Better communication and collaboration between departments and other stakeholders can break barriers between departments, enable stakeholder to work together to create value, accelerate growth and innovate and enable an organization to gain competitive advantage in a marketplace. Better communication and collaboration will also enable free flow of ideas and information between internal employees and external partners, enable greater access to experts, faster cycle of innovation and rapidly create value, ultimately leading to competitive advantage. A PwC's Global Innovation Survey 2013 shows that innovation leaders collaborate more than the average company with strategic partners, i.e. customers, suppliers, and academics and in some cases may even collaborate with competitors.

Features of social technology such as the ability to connect with colleagues globally, disseminate information quickly and receive immediate feedback and comment, build better relationship - one-to-many relationship makes it an effective tool for communication and collaboration. For example, the ability to connect with people from different departments makes an organization responsive to the demands of its customers. It also eliminates functional barriers and duplication. Using social tools researchers were able to eliminate the difficulty of locating colleagues, which was causing them to work in isolation and duplicate task. Physicians in the same organization were also able to use social tools to communicate experimental drug treatment outcome and side effects to all their stakeholders.

Internally, social technology can help employees scattered across teams and across the world to easily find each other, locate existing information, and co-create products. They can communicate and work collaboratively across dispersed locations. From almost any location employees can initiate projects, form teams, and complete their tasks

Similarly, social tools enhances productivity. Research has demonstrated, that enterprise social technology can decrease the volume of e-mail by as much as 25% and lessen the frequency of physical meetings. Using social technology software like Microsoft Yammer and IBM Connections, many organizations have effectively connected employees in different locations. This has enabled them to collaborate, communicate, share ideas, knowledge, insight and best practices, and manage projects. Furthermore, the use of social technology has significantly reduced travel costs and helped cut training time and cost for new employees.

Shifting communication from one-to-one communication like e-mail to social channels with one-to-many and many to many communication features could save time and money. Employees will be able to communicate cheaper, quicker and faster to a large audience. Again, huge amount of knowledge is locked up in e-mail inboxes which cannot be accessed. With social technology workers have increase speed and easy access to knowledge base and internal expertise, they could save not only the amount of time they spend on writing, reading, and responding to e-mail, but also on the amount of time spent searching for content and expertise, leaving them with more time to engage in more productive activities.

With internal knowledge and information more available on internal networks, a typical interaction worker could reduce information searching time by as much as 35 percent, which will return approximately 6 percent of the workweek to other tasks.

Furthermore, social tools can improve workforce effectiveness. With greater access to internal knowledge base, employees are equip with knowledge to make better decisions and to work together to solve problems. Employees could also save time by having information readily available rather than having to search through their emails for information.

In summary, using social tools internally can increase speed of access to knowledge, reduce communication cost, increase speed of access to internal experts and decreased travel cost resulting in greater employee satisfaction, reduced operational cost and increased revenue.

Externally

A global PwC survey (2013) found that 67% of the most innovative companies employed social media to collaborate externally. For example, through collaboration between Unicharm and P&G, Unicharm was able to bring its innovative hand-held dusters to market faster by relying on the manufacturing, distribution and marketing capacity of P&G. Swiffer Dusters are now sold in 15 global markets. Again, social platforms has enabled collaboration between P&G and stakeholders such as inventors, chemical suppliers and researchers to create innovative products.

Companies are also using social tools to improve external operations. B2B companies are increasingly using social tools to partner with suppliers and other stakeholders to effectively manage procurements, logistics and other supply chain activities. Additionally, Instant communication between parties on B2B supply chains has improved communication and external operations. Also, social tools enables effective coordination of activities among partners in the complex supply chain.

Thirdly, open innovation enabled by social tools through collaboration between internal and external partners are driving growth and productivity. For example, for retail and consumer organizations, open innovation is driving growth through sharing of ideas between internal and external partners. Internal and external partners can connect and share ideas, and get access to a wide network of external expertise and knowledge. Open innovation can even enable collaboration between competitors. For example, open innovation between competitors like Procter & Gamble and Clorox led to the creation of an innovative product Glad trash bag.

Furthermore productivity is also raised through instant communication and collaboration between partners. Through better communication and collaboration, external barriers are broken and information flows freely into the organization bringing in additional knowledge and expertise to accelerate production and increase speed to market.

Businesses and customers can also collaborate on social platforms to co-create products. For example, Starbucks has launched over 300 ideas through external collaboration with customers through social platforms. By listening to customers on social platforms they were able to establish their customers' needs. Furthermore, by creating online communities, consumers were able to share ideas and Starbuck experience, vote for favorites, and interact with Starbucks employees.

In summary social tools can improve collaboration and communication. When done effectively, they can drive innovation and growth and also improve business support functions.

Business Support

As mentioned above, business support functions includes administrative activities such as human resources (HR), procurement, project support, product development, training, finance and accounting.

HR and Talent Management

Social tools can be used to improve business support functions. For example, if you take human resources, it has become a core tool for hiring, with 94% of recruiters (according to Altimeter) using social tools for recruiting in 2013. Most employers use LinkedIn, Twitter, and Facebook to find more high-qualified candidates, build better relationship with potential candidates and to improve their brand.

Social tools have expanded the search for talent. Organizations now have access to a large pool of potential talents worldwide. They can quickly search social media for talents worldwide, identify what skills and talents are available worldwide and the abilities of potential candidates.

Additionally, social tools has improved screening and matching of talents. Traditionally, recruiters will manually read large volumes of candidates' CV to search for specific skills and expertise. This was time consuming, costly and less effective. With social tools recruiters can screen large numbers of profiles quickly to identify potential candidates with specific skills and talents. They can also use their profile, content they have uploaded on their profile, references, or recommendations from existing connection within their social graph to screen potential candidates.

Employers can build better relationship with potential candidates and also build their brand with social media by encouraging current employees to engage with potential job candidates on social media. By developing a relationship with potential candidates and engaging them with targeted contents, organizations can position their brand better and gain a better understanding of their potential candidates.

Furthermore, social tools can be used for personnel tasks i.e. allocating task, orienting new hires and selecting project team members. Social tools can be used to identify suitable candidates for a task. For example, employees can be allocated task based on their expertise and their contributions to solving issues on enterprise social platforms. New employees can quickly identify and connect with staff with relevant skills that they need to quickly settle down quickly. In some organizations, new recruits are given social graph of co-workers and expertise to connect with them and to help them settle down quickly. Using social platforms, companies can quickly identify candidates for geographically dispersed teams based on their profile, skills and experience. Team members can use social tools to collaborate on projects, share knowledge, work on documents simultaneously, and communicate with other remote team members.

Social tools enhance peer to peer learning. For example, employees can share knowledge, collaborate to solve problems and to support each other on social networks. Social tools also support documentation and sharing of results. Results and solutions can be documented and accessed by employees facing similar problems in the future.

Social tools can be used to improve employee satisfaction and to monitor employee progress and achievements. Unlike traditional annual performance management review, management can give instant and ongoing feedback using social tools. On an enterprise social network, management can search for talent management related posts to assess the achievements of an employee and progress of employee. For example, using keywords like 'thanks', 'help', congratulation, 'assisting me to solve this problem', praise etc. management can quickly compile a better employee achievement report on social networks.

Product Development

Product Development which traditionally relied on research and what the organization thought will sell has been enhanced by social tools. Companies are using social tools to crowdsource product ideas. Starbuck and Dell are typical examples of companies that have used social tools to generate and implement new products. Companies can solicit ideas directly from customers by asking for feedback on social media or by listening to their customers' conversations online to determine their needs and make products that meet their needs.

Customer Care

Social tools have become an integral part of many brands' customer support functions. Most companies now have a dedicated Twitter account to answer queries and complaints. For example, Wells Fargo uses "@Ask_WellsFargo" on Twitter to support customer support function. Social tools enables faster response times and it is delivered at a lower cost than call center operation.

Additionally, companies can use social tools to proactively engage potential customers. They can target potential clients by searching for the mention of product related words, for example a company selling baby products can search for the mention of 'birth of baby boy' and or 'birth of baby girl' and proactively congratulate the parents and send them links to specific content that will benefit them. If the customer finds the link beneficial, it can help build trust, drive engagement with the brand and may lead to potential sales.

Training

Business support function like training can be enhanced using social tool. With social business networks enabling effective collaboration across global business, many companies are using this tool to deliver highly effective training program. Key features of this tool include a common platform, a centralized communication platform and the ability to collaborate internally and externally using this tool. Constance Hotels and Resorts and One Kings Lane (home decor business) are examples of companies that have used enterprise social network to deliver training and manage projects. Constance Hotels and Resorts used IBM Connect to connect geographically dispersed employee on one platform to deliver training and to share knowledge. This resulted in improvement in productivity because it enabled training to be delivered efficiently across different location and also deployed 70 percent faster. It also allowed employees to connect and share new knowledge, experience and generate ideas leading to innovative products for the company. By embracing IBM Connection, a collaboration solution, the company has enhanced a business support function such as training, and positioned itself in a stronger position to attract top talent for its company.

Constance Hotel and Resorts: using social media for training
Faced with the challenge of delivering training across different Islands as the company experienced growth, Constance Hotels and Resorts selected a social business network based on IBM® Connections Cloud™ and IBM Verse™ .

Prior to implementing IBM connection and Verse, the company had to fly out to the islands to deliver training sessions, which drove up costs and reduced operational efficiency. Additionally, poor communication made it difficult to get everyone together at the same time for the training; sometimes key staff where on leave or had other commitments and therefore could not attend.

Implementing IBM Connection Cloud and IBM Verse, Constance Hotel and Resorts was able to connect geographically dispersed employees on a central communication platform to deliver effective training. Connections also allowed the company to track vacation and other kinds of leave eliminating the risk of missing key people for training. The outcome was effective training for staff, who are now better equipped than ever to deliver consistent high quality service.

Finance

As stated in the introduction, organizations are divided into different departments for reasons such as specialization, division of labor and efficiency. Although the underlying reason for the division of these functions is the benefits that can be made from specialization and the division of labor, collaboration and co-ordination are also required if an organization is to achieve its objectives.

Collaboration and building effective working partnerships is key to the success of not only the organization, but also to the finance function. Business support function like finance can be improved by using enterprise social networks. Enterprise social networks will enable the finance department to collaborate with other departments and external stakeholders to achieve its goals. Collaboration will provide a centralize system, a single place to manage tasks, content, documents, approvals/authorization and ensure the usage of the right processes. This will help· to record transactions in a uniform way, which leads to a reliable source of transactional data for business intelligence. Additionally, it will save time, for example, tasks such as approval, invoice processes which takes days or weeks can now be done instantly and will take less time to accomplish. The net results is increased efficiency and cost savings.

Collaboration will also ensure quick dissemination of information with capability for feedback and comments, creating a shared knowledge base that is transparent and accessible to all. Furthermore it will improve communication between employees and external stakeholders such as vendors, tax authorities and customers and facilitates decision making.

Consider the finance function, it is central in every organization, yet interwoven with other departments like procurement, sales and HR. By collaborating and partnering with these departments and external agencies, the Finance department is able to achieve its goal of reporting the financial performance of an organization. Some of its duties include, keeping and maintaining financial records, preparing financial accounts, paying wages, paying creditors and preparing financial information and analyze financial performance. Finance cannot work in isolation to achieve its goals.

Therefore, for example, collaborating with HR will enable HR to identify and understand the needs of the Finance department and to deliver services that meet their needs. Looking at the objectives of the two departments, you can see that there is a very common alignment between the objectives of HR and finance, both departments want to recruit, develop and retain competent finance staff in the organization. Using social tools will enable HR and the Finance team to work together to reduce recruitment time and improve the quality of staff recruited. Also, staff capability is fundamental to the success of any finance function, so an effective working relationship between HR and finance is key. Furthermore, collaborating with HR on enterprise social networks will enable HR to create compelling training programs which meet the needs of the finance team. Collaboration will also improve communication and working relationship between the two departments.

Finance and Procurement

Another example is the relationship between Finance and procurement. The procurement function is responsible for buying goods and services for the organization and a large consumer of an organization's cash. As such, it must work together with Finance to ensure that it makes wise decisions in performing its duties. Procurement and Finance also share common goals, including the need to achieve rapid savings and monitor and control external risk factors.

Essentially, social tools will improve business support functions such as recording detailed transaction information, processing invoices, financial reporting and analysis. Using common system will ensure that transactions are recorded accurately, and duplication is also eliminated. Collaborating on a common platform using social tools will improve visibility and ensure process compliance. This will enable Finance to keep a grip on cost and have an insight into the operation of procurement.

Furthermore, accurate recording of data in a uniform way leads to a reliable source of data, which can improve financial reporting and analysis. It can also lead to better operational decisions such as improving operational procurement processes. Again, accurate data can provide better insight for better and more informed decision i.e. the availability of assets and working capital. For example, where accurate financial reports indicate that there is sufficient working capital, Finance can decide to pay invoice earlier and get discount.

Additionally, social tools will improve communication between procurement and finance team and help to build better working relationship between the two teams. Better communication will result in better response time and efficiency. Not only will social tools improve communication between Finance and Procurement function, it will improve communication between procurement staff. Procurement buyers can share information between themselves, keep track of all information gathered during sourcing and share it with co-workers to gather feedback.

Finance and Sales

For Sales to be as effective, the sales team need to have a better relationship with Finance to avoid inefficient business processes that lead to invoicing errors, delays and bad customer service.

Social tools can connect Finance and Sales together to enable them to build better relationship, share up-to-minute data and communicate online. Finance and Sales can work side by side to understand customer credit balances, to invoice more efficiently and accurately, and to collect cash quicker, ultimately improving customer service.

Business support functions relating to Finance and Sales such as recording sales information and order processing can be improved with both teams working together on a common platform towards a common goal. Instant communication will reduce response time and improve order processing and invoicing. Accounts queries can be dealt with more efficiently. Traditionally, sales staff will contact Finance by e-mail regarding invoice queries. With Sales and Finance staff collaborating on a common platform through secure connected sales and finance application, staff have access to up-to-date information and can deal with queries quicker and efficiently. Finance and Sales can work side by side to understand customer credit balances, to invoice more efficiently and accurately, and to collect cash quicker, ultimately improving customer service and the financial position of the company.

Accurate data leads to more accurate forecasting. Better sales forecasting will enable the company to prepare resources to cope for growth such as increase demand and sales.
Visibility between both functions will ensure that issues such as inaccurate billing and non-payment by a customer is identified immediately, and both teams can work together to resolve the issue. Collaboration helps to deliver proactive customer service while ensuring optimal cash flow.

Accounting Departing And Other Department

Accounting departments are often perceived as obstacles to business rather than enablers. Dealing with the accounting department can be frustrating because of the time and limitation they sometimes put on our expenditure. Also, the way most accounting departments are structured and the bureaucratic way of operation often isolates them from other departments and make them irrelevant.

Enterprise social media technologies can offer accounting teams a better way to become more relevant across the business. For example, using Salesforce Chatter, a social enterprise application could enable the accounting department to perform the transactional functions and also collaborate and communicate effectively with other departments enabling them to build trust, removing isolation and improve communication.

Not only can social tools enable the accounting department to collaborate with other departments, it can also facilitate projects by preventing delays.

One of the factors that makes it difficult for projects to meet their deadlines is delay in releasing funds. Social tools can help an organization overcome this challenge by enabling the accounting department to work together with other departments particularly the project team, this brings about transparency, which helps to detect problems or anything that could cause delay early and then rectified it to avoid delays. There is also better co-ordination between departments to facilitate projects and sharing of information. Internal time consuming reports are reduced, and the number of signatures required for capital expenditures is also reduced thereby shortening the time for approval. Accounting tasks i.e. authorization that causes delays can be done faster with social tools and duplication of tasks eliminated. What normally take days or weeks can now be done in minutes or hours, resulting in efficiency and effectiveness.

Embedding social tools into accounting applications will enable the accounting team to engage with other departments and also other department to engage with the accounting team. This will improve communication between departments and increase transparency between departments. Additionally, it will help the Accounting department to be more strategic by gaining a better understanding of what other departments are doing, and also be in a better position to advise on the financial matters and the implications for the whole business.

Social technology will make the accounting department more relevant, more engaged, and it will enable the department to build trust across the business.

Logistics And Operation

Social technology has become a tool for managing logistics and operations. It allows instant communication between different parties on B2B supply chains.

Companies collaborating on social platforms are more responsive to their customer needs and transaction. The connected advantage gives them access to real time visibility and wealth of information across the supply chain to meet the changing customer needs. Retailers also have access to critical information from the supply chain ecosystem which they can utilize to improve their logistics operation and respond effectively to the expectations of their digital customers. For example, for a retailer, collaboration enables an integrated system with partners, which gives access to wealth of information on the supply chain ecosystem, seamless information sharing across fulfilment channels and real-time visibility enabling flexible shipping options for customers. Customers benefit from a wider assortment of products and good customer service as better information flow and real time visibility can be used to improve customer service. Distribution of logistics can also be improved due to visibility, better tracking system, better communication and flexible distribution options using social technology.

CHAPTER 8

Risks

Social technologies have drastically changed the way people interact with their friends, acquaintances and family members. It connects people with people. Many people have gained great personal satisfaction from the relationships they have formed online, the insight they have gained, the communities they have formed through their use of social technologies and the opportunity to effect positive change in their communities.

However, the freedom to contribute in any way and manner, and the ability to remain anonymous on social media creates many risks for individuals. It exposes people to vandalism, bullying, theft and blackmail.

Furthermore, users provide social network operators with their personal information which attackers could hack and use to answer personal knowledge questions and consequently impersonate them. Comments, posts and photographs could be used in a different context to blackmail the user.

Risks to businesses

The use of social technology offers opportunities and also carries considerable risks. It offers companies the opportunity to engage and communicate effectively with all stakeholders, build brand, and also gather information that can alert the board about risks facing the organization. There is also some evidence that social media provides effective early warning to risk. For example, Nestlé first came under criticism in online communities for sourcing palm oil from an Indonesian supplier accused of destroying rainforests. Had the board been monitoring the discussion online, they might be alerted earlier to the risk and moved proactively to address it. In this way, information gathered through social media can supplement the data provided by management regarding key risk factors facing the organization.

Despite offering opportunities to recognize early warning signs, it is difficult, especially for companies to anticipate all the risks posed by social media. For example, financial institutions have had to shut down social media forums due to unanticipated negative feedback; the stock market has been struck by fraudulent social network postings; businesses have suffered brand damage due to negative comments.

Risk from social media is progressively ranked high on board discussions. According to the National Association of Corporate Directors (2014), "risk" ranks third on the list of topics that boards spend the most time discussing, after strategy and financial reporting. Another survey by Grant Thornton, an advisory firm reported that 71 percent of the executives surveyed said their company was concerned about possible risks posed by social media. Despite many firms recognizing the potential negative impact social media can have on their company, 59 percent reported their organization did not have a social media risk assessment plan in place.

As research shows risk is ranked high in corporate discussions, yet recognizing the importance of risk management is not the same as effectively managing risk. Many companies have failed to respond effectively to social media risks despite anticipating the risks.

What Is Risk Management?

Risk management is the process by which an organization anticipates and reduces its exposure to adverse outcomes. Risk management entails identifying events that have the potential to disrupt a company's operations, assessing the likelihood of their occurrence, and taking action to minimize their impact either through prevention or a prepared response.

Some of the risks from social media include:

Proprietary Information: Intellectual Property

Intellectual property (IP), a driving force for innovation, competition and growth of businesses is vital to the 21st-century company and constitute more than 80 percent of a single company's value today. It may be some of the reasons why thieves are interested in stealing this information from companies.

Many factors have contributed to the rise in this crime. For example, advancement in technology, rapid globalization and the anonymous nature of the internet has made theft easier, and increasingly difficult to protect trade secrets. The use of advanced technologies like social media has increased the risks, a McKinsey survey reported that 55 percent of executives said that the use of social technologies significantly increased the risk of confidential information being leaked.

Historically, trade secrets were kept in filing cabinets, but with digitization, information is now kept in the form of data on computers which can be hacked and information stolen. Criminals can attack cyber networks from anywhere in relative anonymity and can steal trade secrets such as drug trial data, potential cure for a disease, product formula, unique design or copyrighted data.

Secondly, the speed and reach of social technologies makes it easy to disseminate intellectual property. A McKinsey survey indicated that 40 percent of executives felt that the use of social technologies significantly increased the risk of distributing intellectual property inappropriately. Users can instantly share protected information faster and more easily on social media including platforms like Napster and Bit Torrent. The anonymous nature of the internet also makes it difficult to track the source of leaked information and information can spread so rapidly that it may be difficult to protect lost or stolen information.

Theft of IP can be detrimental to a company. For example, it might quickly lead to reputation damage of brand, loss of customers and poor credit ratings. It could also deprive a company from first-to-market advantage, loss of revenue and profitability, or in some cases, losing entire lines of business to competitors or fake retailers.

Cyber criminals are increasingly becoming more sophisticated in their crime, but often having a robust and well-implemented cybersecurity and data management/protection strategy, with a contingency plan in the case of an event will mitigate the risk.

Workers Productivity.

There is also the risk that workers' productivity may be impacted. A McKinsey's social technology survey found that 40 percent of employers were worried that social technology distracted employees from their core tasks. It is possible that some workers will spend time on non-work related discussion, leaving them with less time to focus on their main tasks. Having a policy which outline what is permitted will improve productivity and enable employees to additionally enjoy some of the benefits of social media i.e. access to important information and ideas which will ultimately improve their productivity. Some companies have policies which restrict discussion on work related topics.

Reputational/Brand Risk

Reputation and brand risk is the most often discussed and most serious one, according to the 2014 RiskTech100 report. One of the reasons it may occur, may be due to lack of absolute control of staff and therefore, content and quality of external communication resulting in serious brand and reputational damage. Negative exposure to social media sites, or inappropriate or unauthorized action in the company's name, can result in loss of trust and revenues. Many examples can be cited relating to this. For example, Domino Pizza experienced a drop in sales when two of its employees posted a video of themselves violating health codes when preparing an order. In some situations, employees have used social technology to express hostility about their organization or attack management.

Another reason may be due to the speed and reach of social media. Social networks can vastly accelerate the spread of information either positive, negative, true or false about a brand. The broad reach, speed and real-time interaction that makes social media a powerful tool for marketing and advertising can also augment and accelerate risks. These key features of social media have significantly changed the way in which damage is imposed on a company's brand both in terms of speed and scope. Before social media, a negative comment remained within friends and acquaintances or on internet message boards. With social media, a negative comment on Facebook or Twitter can be re-tweeted, reposted and viewed by millions of people within a short time and in some cases reach media outlets as happened with Kevin Smith's tweet, when he was removed from Southwest Airlines flight, because he was too large to fit in a single seat. The reputational damage, financial cost including impaired goodwill from a negative comment on social media can reach astronomical levels within a short time.

Furthermore, an organization may face liability, if its employees criticizes a competitor through social media and the identity of the employee is discovered. Additionally, there is the risk that social media can be used to harass staff. The ability to remain anonymous on social media makes it easier for employees to harass colleague and attack management. Also, employees or critics outside the organization can use social platforms to share negative information and opinions about the organization, potentially doing serious damage to the reputation of the organization or its brands.

Equally, reputational risk can affect business operation. A survey by the Economist Intelligence Unit (EIU) indicates that leading European managers consider reputational risk as a primary threat to business operations and the market value of their organizations. For example, financial institutions have had to shut down their social media forums due to negative comments. Reputation risk can also occur through inappropriate data sharing and misuse or release of sensitive or restricted information. This can affect trust and loyalty of stakeholders (particularly customers), consequently affecting product demand and eventually market share, value, competitiveness and operation.

Despite realizing the importance of reputation risk, organizations continue to neglect reputation risk management strategies. Businesses can use strategies such as policies, technology to minimize risks. For example, having policies governing the use and access to data i.e. Data Protection policies, installing effective systems and applications to improve data management and monitoring of social media activities and swift response using social media in response to negative comments that may damage the reputation of an organization. A prompt and creative response to a negative comments may even change negative sentiments into positive sentiments. If negative comments about an organization goes unchecked or unanswered for a long time, the situation may worsen and become difficult to correct.

Internally, some businesses monitor internal social networks use to minimize reputational damage from negative comments or unauthorized access (audit trail) by employees. Such an approach, can sometimes prevent honest and open communication, which is necessary to improve productivity. Having honest and unfiltered feedback also helps to build trust with management. Feedback from employees can be used to improve products and operations in the company.

Financial Loss Due To Malware

There is also the risk of financial loss due to false transaction which may occur by clicking on a false link. It is common to share and send links to friends and family on social media. Hackers send malicious links to users which tricks them into fraudulent transactions. They send users links to interesting videos and useful information, in some cases they may use adverts. When users click on the links, it installs hidden software on their devices, which enables the hackers to steal data and personal information of the user as well as corporate information on the user's computer. Avoiding clicking links from unknown source could help minimize this risk.

Fraud

Fraud is a major problem and many major brands and news outlets have experienced it. Fraudsters misrepresent organizations and post fake messages that will favor them. They also post links to encourage users to visit harmful sites so that they can inject viruses into their computer and mobile phones.

The viral nature of social media makes it easy to commit fraud and difficult to control fraud as information goes viral so quickly on social media making it easy to achieve intended outcome. For example, hackers can falsely represent organizations on social media and post fake information which can go viral speeding up the intended outcome. A typical example, is the impact of the Associated Press hackers on the Dow Jones. The Dow Jones Industrial Average fell about 150 points when hackers presenting as the Associated Press on twitter posted a false story, which caused a loss of approximately $150 billion in market value within minutes. In other cases, hackers misrepresenting a company have posted fake announcements with extraordinary financial news, enabling them to profit from a rise in the company's stock price.

Another method is the use of links. Hackers use links i.e. bit.ly links to trick users to visiting harmful sites or to inject viruses into their computers. They can easily install spywares into the user's device, which can enable them to retrieve the user's password remotely by sending downloadable links to users. Some other scams involves using the messaging capabilities within social media platforms to conduct computer attacks. The best way to avoid being a victim, is to never click on links unless you're sure of the actual source.

In another recent trend, hackers are establishing second Facebook pages for people and companies, building relationships and creating situations to make it easier for people to divulge important information like their password, credit card details etc.

Finally, there is the risk of identity theft. This is because most social media sites require users to provide personal information to register with the site. Fraudsters tend to gather their victims' personal information from the information available on the social media sites. They hack their victim's e-mail account by simply using personal information available on social media profile.

Privacy Violations

Privacy violation is equally rated high on the list of risks for companies using social technology. Users often share intimate details about themselves on social platforms i.e. e-mails, telephone numbers, preferences, interests, hobbies, relationship status, likes and dislikes and links (friendship, group membership, social browsing history). Marketers see this an opportunity to collect information that would enable them to personalize their services to users and effectively target their audience. There is the possibility they may use it inappropriately. Inappropriate use of personal data may be considered a breach of privacy and may result in regulatory sanctions against the company.

Security breaches may sometimes be unintentional, for example it may occur through a software bug allowing users' information to be shared publicly as happened with Facebook users in 2013, resulting in users' information such as contact details and addresses being shared publicly, or an employee over-disclosure of personal life events, which flows into professional life events leading to disclosure of client's information on social media. For example, employees may tweet about an interesting project they are doing with good intent, but a corporate spy might be able to put several information together to develop a picture about a company's product in progress.

Secondly, user privacy can be violated through a technique called "data scraping." This is a method of tracking people's activities online and gathering personal data from their use of social media sites as well as online sites. Research companies use this technique to gather personal information about people to sell to companies for marketing purpose.

Consumer privacy can again be violated through phishing schemes (links) that looks genuine asking users to reset password or reveal personal details, resulting in users revealing their passwords. Since most people use the same password for different accounts it may result in access to corporate networks.

Privacy violation may also occur with (LBS) location based social networks i.e. Gowalla, Foursquare, and Google Latitude, which uses global positioning system (GPS), to track user's location with other vital features such as instant messaging. Foursquare users for example, use the platform to let friends know where they are and what they're doing. There is the risk that information users publish on these platforms could be used to track their whereabouts and in some cases stalk them.

Furthermore, applications built on LBS could be used to reveal the identity of users as happened with the Girls Around Me app. The app which was built on Foursquare API, filters people by geographical position and gender and links with Facebook to display the user's picture. This threatens user's privacy and safety. Foursquare has since fixed this problem. However people and organizations need to be careful about the information they share on such platforms.

Risks Management/Mitigating Risks

As noted there are considerable risks in using social media. Financial institutions have had to shut down social media forums due to unanticipated negative feedback. The inability to protect users from malicious agents has led to sensitive and confidential information being made public. If these risks are not effectively mitigated, they can lead to serious negative consequences including fraud, intellectual property loss, financial loss, privacy violations and failure to comply with laws and regulations. A key goal of effective risk management is to minimize the occurrence of risks, as well as to improve the capabilities and capacities for handling risks in an organization. This may involve improving the capacity and capability of all staff or the people responsible for handling risks through training and raising awareness, improving the processes and structures for handling risks, using technology to improve the efficiency of the risks handling processes.

Governance/Policy

Creating new structures, policies and accountabilities for managing social media risks. Policies should be flexible and responsive to the rapidly changing social media environment. It is important to have well-defined roles and accountabilities for each type of social media risk across functional areas to ensure accountability. For example, define roles and responsibilities for reputational risks (managed by the marketing department), privacy and violation (managed by the legal department), fraud (managed by the Audit) etc. It is equally important for different functional areas to work together and co-ordinate activities especially in large organizations, to avoid duplication of efforts and sending out conflicting messages. This may involve sharing information across functions. Equally important is the need to have a well-defined escalation pathway and procedures for managing crisis i.e. appoint someone who will be responsible for making ultimate decisions about social media risks, managing risks and handling any crises that may arise.

Secondly, continuously monitoring social media risks and reporting risks from different functional areas to detect early warning signs and then reporting any issues to social media risk manager, who then reports to senior management. For example, HR may focus on identifying, assessing and managing risks on LinkedIn, Marketing may focus on Facebook and Twitter, and legal may focus on monitoring e-mails traffic for issues of liabilities. They then report any issue to the social media manager. Continuous monitoring will ensure early detection of problems and companies can take quick steps to fix the problem. Technology can be used to enhance the monitoring process, for example, web crawlers and analytic tools can be used to analyze sentiments and to detect reference to a company, determine the nature of the reference i.e. whether positive or negative, the context i.e. quality or customer care issues and report back. In this way, reputational risks can be identified quicker and counter-actions put in place quickly.

Using Technology

Thirdly, companies could improve the effectiveness of their IT systems to manage social media risks. For example, using advanced technology to improve data storage, privacy, security, management and analysis of data, reporting and using new technologies to monitor social media sites to mitigating risks. Several analytic tools (i.e. NetBase, IBM Watson Analytics) now exist for mining and analyzing social media data; Web crawlers can also be used to extract user data from social media. The data can be analyzed to help make more informed decisions. Companies can also benefit from using these data mining tools to improve business intelligence and to detect user sentiments.

Sentiments analysis provide early warning of risks which can damage a company's brands. Companies can take proactive measures to address those risks. Additionally, companies can use text analytic engines to find pattern in data to provide them with insights and enable them to make better decisions. Furthermore, improvements in the management and analysis of data could enable companies to produce more efficient and timely reports which would enable management to make better decisions about risks.

Transferring Risks

Companies could also transfer some or all the risks elsewhere i.e. insuring against risks. Some companies may have business insurance packages which covers some or all of the risks identified. It is worth taking a careful look at what you have to check whether it is enough to insure you against social media risks.

Culture change/Training

People's behavior must change to manage risk effectively. Improving data management systems, policies and technology is not enough to mitigating social media risks. You need people to work with the technology to improve risk management, you also need people to implement the desired change to manage risks effectively. This requires employees to be knowledgeable about risks and understand their role in mitigating risks. With support from senior management, the risk manager can create a risk aware culture. A culture where employees understand the risks of social media, how their actions can expose the company to risks, how to avoid those risks and how to report risks. The risk manager could also continuously communicate with staff to explain how the business is being exposed to social media risks and how each individual can contribute to managing those risks. This requires employee training. Training will provide employees with knowledge and guidance and an understanding of their role in mitigating risks.

CHAPTER 9

Strategy: Creating A Strategy

A strategy defines how to achieve a goals. It is a plan or systematic steps a company takes to achieve its goal. Social media strategy is therefore the approach or plan a company takes to achieve its social media goals. A strategy is an important element of a successful social media program.

A report by Smartsights.com 'Managing Digital Marketing 2015', shows that 50% of marketers have active digital marketing programs, but no defined strategy. Although these companies are experiencing some degree of success, for example they have decent numbers of fans, likes and followers, it does not mean that their social media strategy is working. Many of them have failed to achieve their ultimate goal of converting their fans into buyers or to achieve their goal.

It is therefore important for a company to have a social media strategy. This is because a social media strategy will show how the company intends to achieve its social media goals: For example, if the goal of a company is to increase profit by increasing its customer base through social media, its social media strategy will show how it intends to this i.e. by what percentage, its target audience, and through which social media channel. A strategy gives the company an opportunity to think carefully about how it will achieve its goals, the resources it will need, the choices it will make, the tools, the channels it will use and how to measure success.

Without specific goals, it is difficult to know exactly what you need to do online, and later to measure how successful you are. A good strategy will benchmark your activity, clearly set out what goals you need to achieve online, and guide your actions. It will also be a measure by which you determine whether you're succeeding or failing. Furthermore, creating a written strategy enables companies to identify any issues and also address crucial questions, as well as formulate a powerful online value proposition, define the target audience, and carefully consider all the other elements of an effective digital programme.

There is no one-size-fits-all social media strategy, because what worked for one company may not work for another. For example, what worked for Dell, may not work for Primark.

The following steps will guide you to maximize your social media effectiveness online.

Creating a Strategy

1. Assessing and integrating with your organization's current social media capability

It is important to assess your current capability especially if you already have a social media site. By assessing your current social media capability, you are able to take stock of what you already have, so that you don't duplicate or waste time, money and effort doing the same things. It will also help to ensure consistency across the organization. When J&J's vice president was asked to start the company's Digital Centre of Excellence, a capability assessment revealed that the company had hundreds of different websites and digital platforms operating globally. Identifying existing websites and working towards integrating all the websites and digital platforms ensured consistent communication across the world for a company with multiple brands in multiple regions, and also helped to identify important stakeholders to work with to establish the center.

Before you start planning it is important that you begin by assessing your current organizational activity and interest. This will help you to identify internal stakeholders or departments (i.e. marketing/communication department) that you may need to engage with. You also need to establish:

- Whether there are existing social media policies and guidelines.
- Whether some departments or employees already use social media and what platforms and monitoring tools they are using.
- Assess the training needs of internal stakeholders - are there existing social media training programmes?
- Internal resources that could support the development or delivery of social media strategy i.e. identify internal social media staff.
- Identify issues or barriers i.e. legislation

Completing the assessment will help you to identify resources and barriers relating to existing social media programme. It will also enable you to identify those capabilities and capacities in your organization that can help you to deliver a social media strategy. For example, it will help identify the social media assets and needs of internal stakeholders i.e. staff. The results of such assessments could be used to shape the strategy development process.

For example, the assessment process may reveal whether existing staffs have social media skills or not, or whether a social media policy exists. The results of the assessment can serve as input for shaping the strategy development process. Existing social media policy could be updated to reflect the new strategy, instead of writing a new policy; existing staffs with social media skills will require less or no training; existing platform could be evaluated to see whether it meets the organization's social media goal. If not, a new policy and platform will be created and staffs will be provided full training.

2. Listening

The primary goal of listening is to identify the needs of the consumer and to learn about their social behavior. Before Dell launched its first social media presence in 2006, the company began by listening for nine months to what people were writing on blogs and discussion forums about Dell. Another example, is GE. At GE, many business departments began their social business journey by listening to their customers or using insight conducted through a combination of digital market research, online surveys, and focus groups.

It is important to listen to what consumers are saying about your company and brand so that you can gain a deeper understanding of your customers and build products that meets their needs. For example, before social media, insurance company USAA have for years been anticipating customer needs, with social media tools they were able listen to customers to determine their needs rather than anticipate their needs, engage with them and develop products that meets their needs.

Traditional survey, focus groups or "ask-based" research can provide feedback and help companies anticipate needs but unable to capture passion. Social listening is vital to understanding the passion and sentiments of consumers online, which traditional survey and questionnaire cannot capture. Kraft Foods used Nielsen's social listening frameworks to listen and obtain feedback from consumers. Before entering the burger market, Kraft had extensive knowledge of the cheese market but lacked enough knowledge and understanding about the cheeseburger market. By listening to consumers online, it was able to establish what consumers where saying about its brand regarding cheese and other products such as cheeseburger. It was also able to obtain consumer sentiments, preference, product trends, emerging flavours and consumer profiles about the new market that it intended to enter. Nielsen framework enabled Kraft to focus in on different themes such as health and wellness, sustainability, dinner, and even on occasions like getting out of the house in the morning.

You can use social media as a research tool to find out what information is already being shared about your organization and products and to identify conversation topics and people. Listening to and evaluating conversations on social media can also help to gather insights, identify gaps in messaging and understand what people care about, which in turn will help to plan content and align messages with audience. Additionally, using web analytic tools, can help identify different groups that engage in topics that are of interest to the organization and brand.

It is also important to select the right monitoring tool for listening to consumer conversation. Ideally, a tool that has the capacity to listen to conversation in different languages. There are many social media platforms online, with conversations in different languages. This makes it difficult to monitor all that is being said about a company and brand globally. Furthermore, understanding comments in different languages, analysing or clarifying the (geographic) scope of a topic, ensuring that your message reach your target audience can be challenging.

There are wide varieties of social media monitoring and analysis tools that can help overcome these challenges. These tools are designed to listen in on topical discussions, map the location of contributors, monitor contributions in multiple languages, and identify key influencers. The essential qualities of a good tool is one that is capable of monitoring and analysing conversation and also useful for engaging clients. In selecting a monitoring tool, a good starting point is to establish which social media sites are monitored by the tool and whether these sites are relevant to you. A tool for monitoring professional websites like LinkedIn will not be suitable for monitoring a retail brand. Also, some tools provide content management and publishing functionality as well as analytics and they cover a number of useful activities too.

Examples of Social Analytic Tools

Social analytic tools performs different functions i.e. listening, monitoring, publishing and analyzing social media activities. Each tool is unique and may not perform all functions listed above. Examples of tools include Radian6, HootSuite, Brandwatch, Engagor, Sysomos, Talkwalker, Trackur and Twitalyzer, Klout, Social Mention, Twitter Analytics, Facebook Insights, TweetDeck, and Keyhole.

Hootsuite is useful for listening, analyzing topics and monitoring trends. A free version (with limited features) is available for download.

Radian6 is useful for reviewing historical data from a number of social media sites. Radian6 is also capable of searching in over 32 different languages and gives the option to select geographical regions for searches. It is not free.

Engagor enables organizations to listen, monitor and analyze what is being said about them. Engagor provides a variety of functions which other products don't have. For example, it supports multiple users, tag conversations, perform analyses, identify influencers, and publish across multiple platforms. It also keeps track of related information shared on social networks, news sites, blogs, and forums. It is not free.

3. Set goals and objectives

What is your purpose? Why do you want to use social media? Your answer will shape your goals and objectives. You may want to use social media to engage with your customers, improve sales, raise awareness of your brand, to increase your customer base or to communicate your values.

Define the goals and objectives for your social media strategy based on your organizational goals and the information gathered through listening. The most important ingredients for a successful social business strategy are clear alignment of objective with the strategic business goals of an organization and executive support that enables execution of the strategy.

For example, for a public health organization, the objective to share public health information with as many people as possible is aligned with the overall goal or strategy of the public health organization. Aligning social media objectives with organizational objectives will enable social media staff to gain support from senior management. One of the biggest cause of social media strategy failure is lack of alignment with business objectives. Aligned objectives contributes to the success of an organization. Social media managers are more likely to get approval or executive buy-in and investment if their objectives are aligned with the organization's goal. Non-aligned objectives may be considered a distraction, and therefore less likely to get the full attention of executives or senior management. Without internal support and access to resources your social media strategy will struggle to succeed.

Use the SMART framework when setting your goals. This means that each objective must be specific, measurable, achievable, realistic, and time-bound.

- Specific: What is your objective? Example of specific objective - increase revenue through sales by 10%.
- Measurable: How will you measure progress? - The target for each week is at least 100 likes and 20 comments.
- Achievable: Can the objectives be achieved with the current resources, capabilities, capacities? Yes, will require growing customer base on popular social media sites i.e. Facebook and Instagram.
- Realistic: Are the objectives actually possible to attain, and if so, what evidence is available? –Yes, similar results have been achieved by other retailers with same or limited resources.
- Time-based: When do you expect to achieve your objectives – achieved within a year.

Example of a SMART Objective

Goal: increase revenue
Objective: One of the objective which will contribute to reaching the goal of increasing revenue is to increase sales of red wine by 10% within a year, by engaging with red wine consumers on Facebook and Instagram. Increase sales is aligned with the overall goal of increasing the revenue of the organization.
How are we going to achieve this? We will run a campaign on Facebook and Instagram that will enable us to increase our brand awareness, increase our existing customers and consequently increase sales. For Facebook we will offer discount coupons to new connections on Facebook on their first online purchase and £5 off next online purchase to any user who shares our offers this year. For Instagram we will share photos that communicate our company's culture and products. This will increase awareness and increase exposure of our products. We will do this by posting 5 photos a week. The

target for measuring our success each week is to get at least 100 likes and 20 comments.

There are 3 ways a retailer can increase sales:

- Frequency - get existing customers to buy from you more often – by offering existing customers coupons and discount with links to the company's website.
- Acquire new customers – by growing audience on social media – raise awareness of the product. Engage with followers. Offer discount coupons to new connections on Facebook on their first online purchase.
- Get existing customers to spend more with you every time they buy something – offering other related products to customers every time they buy from you.

4.   Identify Your Target Audience

You need to identify your target market so you can target your audience with the right message. Who are your target audience? Are you targeting Millennials, mums with young children, dads, or senior executives nearing retirement? What are they doing on social media, and where are they doing it? You could find answers to these questions:

- Who are your customers? By creating your target audience profile i.e. create a buyer personas.
  Create a detailed profile of your ideal customer/client. How old are they? Female or Male? What is their income? Do they have children? What do they like or dislike? What motivates them? Where do they spend their time online?

- Where are your customers? By checking out stats from Pew Research that break down the demographics of each social network or by conducting a survey to ask current customers. You could also ask your customers:

  Which social media websites do they visit or belong to? • Which social media sites do they log onto regularly? How often? • Which social media sites do they post to, and how often? • Find out their age, gender, household income and education level?

- You could also use social media listening tools.

Match your target audience profile/buyer persona to the stats from Pew Research and answers to your survey to select the platform that matches your audience profile/buyer persona. For example if your buyer persona is young and under 30 years you may consider choosing Instagram. If your target audience are females you may consider Pinterest.

Using social listening tool i.e. Tracx, Nikon realized that 66 percent of its audience on social media are male and only 33 percent are female, and the age group discussing its products is between 20 and 30 years. Tracx also informs Nikon which users have recently enrolled in a photography class. Using this insight, Nikon was able to target its marketing towards its younger male audience and send personalized offerings to jump-start sales.

Another example, is Mercedes-Benz, a legendary brand previously associated with older buyers. The company wanted to reach and embrace a new generation of luxury drivers at a time when most car shoppers wanted to do more of their consideration online. Mercedes-Benz's goal was to reach Millennials, therefore working in partnership with Razorfish, it was able to figure out its target audience and where they were active on social media. With that insight, it was able to target under 35 year old with its CLA model on Instagram to appeal to an up-and-coming generation.

5. Map your social media goals/objectives to your social media key performance indicators (KPI) Link your goals to social media key KPI. If your goal is to improve brand awareness, measure the number of followers/fans, if your goal is to drive sales online – you can measure clicks-through from social platforms to purchase.

Example

Goal/Objective: Improved brand awareness

Link to social metrics that measure: social exposure, influence and engagement.

Measure Social Exposure:

Twitter/Facebook: Measure the number of followers/fans, comments, likes, shares, unique website visits referred from social media content and the number of retweets on Facebook and twitter. Compare the month-over-month growth rate of these metrics so that you can determine where you're seeing the most growth. TweetReach is a great free tool for measuring some of these metrics on Twitter.

YouTube: Measure the number of views for videos tied to a promotion or specific period of time, such as weekly/monthly, page ranking on key terms from YouTube and the total number of subscribers. Social media likes and shares, or unique website visits referred from social media content.

Blog: Measure the number of visitors who viewed the posts for a promotion or a specific period of time.

Measuring Engagement:

- Twitter: Measure the number of people/number of times your links were clicked, your message was retweeted, your hashtag was used and also track @replies to campaigns.

- Facebook: Measure the number of times your links were clicked and your messages were liked or commented on.

- YouTube: Measure the number of comments on your video, the number of times it was rated, the number of times it was shared and the number of new subscribers.

- Blog: Measure the number of comments, the number of subscribers generated and the number of times the posts were shared and "where" they were shared (i.e., Facebook, Twitter, email, etc.).

Some useful tools Radian 6, Biz360 and TweetEffect.

Measuring Influence

Measuring influence will determine whether people are ecstatic about your brand or not. You can measure the number of positive sentiments or the number of complaints. Measure metrics such as customer satisfaction, share of your message vs competitors, number of brand evangelists and sentiments (the number of positive, neutral or negative sentiments for your campaign or brand). You can also measure customer feedback, use top influencers' report or tools like Twitalyzer, Social Mention, Radian 6, ScoutLabs or Klout which measures an individual's online impact.

Other KPI Measurements

For measuring sales – use Google Analytics Social Reports to measure clicks-through from social platforms to purchase. Google Analytics Social Reports is a useful tool for this. It provides a breaking down of social traffic and assigns monetary value to website conversions such as sales or lead generation.

6.   Establish Rules

Once you have identified your objectives, target audience and map your key performance indicators, you may want to establish rules:

Social Media Policy

Develop formal policies and guidelines for all staff.

Clear social media policies for staff are essential to ensure that employees understand what is expected of them when using social media. This may include which type of content can be shared and when.

What should be included in the social media policy?

What's your employee policy on social networks? What should your policy document contain? You can include what can and cannot be published, tone of voice & language principles, privacy principles, non-disclosure principles and general customer service standards. Staff should exercise caution and discretion i.e. non-divulgence of any information that has not yet been made public. Having clear social media policy in place and ensuring staff are briefed or trained can improve compliance and help you achieve meaningful and engaging social media content.

Identify Risks Issues

In developing your social media policies, consideration should be given to risks that may arise from social media activity and how they should be addressed. For example, address issues relating to risks in your policy i.e. breaches of customer's privacy, confidentiality, inappropriate post? Issues of confidentiality and disclosure are critical in establishing what can be revealed and what must be withheld when communicating on any social media sites. For example, at pharmaceutical companies, employees must be informed that trade secrets are proprietary information, therefore, cannot be disseminated on social media sites. Some organizations may involve legal staff, marketing and information and financial staff in drafting, executing and updating social media policy.

The following approaches are advisable:

- Compliance with existing privacy and data protection policies.
- Procedures on how to deal with the escalation of issues and possible reputational damage.
- Procedures for the correction of mistakes and for addressing the accidental release of sensitive information or misinformation.

7. Set up team roles and responsibilities: Who will carry out the activities?

You need to have the right staff who can execute your social media strategy properly, and understand the importance of upholding the standards of your brand. First, consider existing staff with social media skills. If not, consider providing your staff with appropriate training or recruiting new staff with the required skills.

From your goals and objectives and the social media tools you are going to use, identify the tasks you will need to perform to achieve your goals.

Assign roles and responsibilities to staff. Ideally, there should be someone to take charge of social media i.e. social media manager who should have the authority to make decisions (in line with their organization's policy) and also assign and delegate responsibilities to others.

Some examples of tasks/responsibilities for a social media manager include:

- Developing, updating and implementing social media strategies.
- Regular monitoring and measurement of key performance indicators.
- Managing social media team.
- Coordinating social media activities.
- Liaising with internal and external departments.

Social Media Administrator

- Monitoring social media sites daily and responding to comments/enquiries by liaising with the appropriate department.
- Posting/updating content on sites three times per week.

- Managing queries and forwarding queries to the appropriate team/member of staff.

How will staff be trained?

It is important to ensure that staff members are fully trained before granting them access to the organization's social media feeds. They also need to be aware of your social media policies so they know what can be shared and published. Training may include how to listen, write, post messages and on social media policies. Conducting a training needs analysis is important to identify the training and development needs of your staff. Consider whether you can deliver training internally by using in-house resources and/or expertise or external agencies.

8. Plan your social media site and content

Which social media platforms should be used?

Decide on which social media platforms to use. When it comes to choosing which social media platforms to use, select those that offer the best potential for reaching your ideal audience. Each platform has its own merits, therefore the platform you choose to deliver your content matters: **Twitter** for example, is best for sharing short, current updates, **YouTube** is good for delivering video content, **LinkedIn** for professional engagement, **Instagram** is good for reaching a younger audience with pictures, and **Snapchat** have younger audiences with multimedia and high engagement rates. **Pinterest** is good for communication via visually rich imagery and has a large female audience. For best result, engage the target audience on the channels they use with material that is unique to the channel.

Think about how you can deliver real value to your audience. Don't limit yourself to one type of media – a mix of videos, guides, tips, infographics and other styles will engage your potential customers more effectively.

You should also identify influencers who can reach your target audience. Good bloggers command high levels of trust to their readers and are indispensable in creating buzz around your brand and products i.e. www.tomoson.com

Also select social channels that fit your brand's message, type of content, and target audience. For example, Mercedes-Benz used Instagram to target millennial audience. Instagram is good for reaching the younger audience with pictures. Razorfish, Mercedes's digital agency selected five of the best photographers on Instagram and gave them five days each to drive a CLA and document the results. The photographer with the most likes won the vehicle. The campaign generated 150 distinct assets for the brand, showing off the CLA in the light of a young driver's life. The campaign also generated 87,000,000 organic Instagram impressions, 2,000,000 likes, and millions more viewing coverage of the campaign beyond the platform and breaking sales records.

You can use more than one accounts on a particular platform to engage with your audience. For example, you could use a main corporate Twitter account to engage with a wide audience, for overall visibility of the organization and for sharing information ; and another separate Twitter account for more specific issues or events i.e. complaints, sales etc.

How will the content be managed?

Content is key. Good content attracts people to social media channels and results in repeat visits which may translate into sales. Therefore, create social media content that drives engagement. What are your target consumer looking for? Regularly produce fresh and relevant content that meet their need. Maintain consistent appearance and provide consistent, valid and authentic information. Create things that your audience will find valuable and helpful or entertaining. For example, an automaker may create "how to articles" to help car users maintain their cars. B&Q, the DIY and home improvements company has created some lovely YouTube content to guide customers through the different ways they can use their products, British high-end fashion house Burberry, also uses social media to show off their new collections and generate user interest and feedback.

You will also need to consider how to maintain a 24/7 presence on social media, as replies, comments, queries, could pop up at any time. Equip staff to be responsive; you can provide staffs with mobile phones which will enable them to access and respond to messages 24/7. Queries that cannot be dealt with immediately can be put on hold and users assured that their queries will be responded to within a specified period of time.

The tone of voice when creating messages on social media is very important. It is better to use plain language and an authoritative tone, without being be too formal. Use a conversational style, be friendly, approachable, flexible, adaptable, honest and responsive.

Use more images, Infographics, charts or a graphs. A picture is better than thousands of words. Social media updates that include images outperform those without. It is also important to keep a library of materials or and records of what has been shared in the past to enable users to review what they have shared in the past.

To maintain an ongoing presence on social media, you will need to deliver fresh content on a regular basis.

9. Get Started

Set up your page/profile/blog on the social media site(s) you have chosen for your message/target audience. If this is your first time, start small and gradually build up your social media presence. This gives you the opportunity to assess what works well and what needs to be done better. Once this has become clear, you can scale up activities. Start sharing key messages with target audiences.

Build your audience: focus on providing your audience with quality, useful and entertaining content. If your audience like your content, they will share with their contacts and your audience will grow. Engage your target audience on the channels they use with material that is unique to the channel. Be open, transparent and honest with your audience.

10. Review: Measure Outputs

Monitor and measure the impact of your strategies

- Measure your achievements against your objectives.

Consider what has worked and what hasn't. Measuring success is important, as it enables you to compare your achievements against your objectives, helps you to identify weaker areas and also gives you the opportunity to adjust and improve your social media strategy.

- Measure how well your campaign is doing?

How many likes/shares or comments you have received. Are you reaching your goal of increasing sales or expanding your customer base? (How many new subscribers have registered with you this week/month?), How many new/repeat customers did you receive? How many customers visited your website? Is your strategy effective? If not, how can you modify your strategy to get a better result?

- The best way to discover this information is to use social monitoring tools such as Radian6 from Salesforce.com, Hootsuite, HubSpot, Klout, Adobe Digital Marketing (offers tracking services, including components for Facebook and Twitter). SocialMention – (provides real-time social media search and analysis); TweetDeck – free personal browser to stay connected with Twitter, Facebook and LinkedIn all at once, Twitter Analytics, Facebook Insights or Keyhole. These monitoring tools will help you to monitor and measure your social media metrics. Some of the monitoring tools may not be for commercial purposes, so check with the vendor or website.

Does the results clearly show how the organization is progressing against the identified social media strategy and objectives?

Monitoring your social media metrics is an ongoing process, therefore, you will have to be continually evaluating your strategy to identify weaker areas which need to be addressed and strengthened them.

This Ten-step social media framework isn't everything you need, but it is a good start.

CHAPTER 10

The Consumer's Journey To Purchase

Social Media is playing significant role in the consumer's journey to purchase. According to Gartner, 74% of consumers rely on social networks on their journey to purchase an item. Fewer consumers are now purchasing items as a direct result of traditional advertising such as television adverts or billboards. Instead, peer recommendations heavily influence shopping behavior throughout the different stages of the consumer journey i.e. awareness, consideration, during shopping and post purchase.

Another study by vision critical also indicates that 4 in 10 social media users have purchased an item online or in-store after sharing or favouriting it on Twitter, Facebook or Pinterest. Social media not only drives people to make online purchases, it also drives an equal volume of in-store sales. With an estimated 2.34 billion worldwide users (according to Statista.com (2017), expected to grow to some 2.95 billion by 2020, social media presents an opportunity for retailers to influence a great number of consumers on their path to purchase. Research shows that people who follow brands on Twitter are 67% more likely to buy a product post-connection and 79% are more likely to recommend a product post-connection. This is a great opportunity for retailers to engage with consumers to influence them on their path to purchase. Retailers who take time to understand the twists and turns consumers take on their path to purchase will capture their attention and ultimately their money and make profit.

The path to purchase

The 'path to purchase' is not a new concept. Although it has significantly evolved over the years due to the internet and digital innovation, the journey itself hasn't change. Consumers still experience the same stages of awareness, consideration, conversion and evaluation.

Stage 1: Awareness

Awareness is the initial stage, when consumers first become aware of the product or have a desire for the product. Awareness can be triggered by adverts, social media, online review, blog, word of mouth or recommendation from a friend or family. Among these triggers, social media is increasing playing a key role. For example, 13% of respondent of KPMG survey stated that they became aware of a product through social media. A Vision critical study also noted that 10% of shoppers who pinned items on Pinterest before buying discovered the item by searching on Pinterest. 72% also found the item by browsing a stranger's Pinterest board or stream, a friend's Pinterest board or stream, a retailer's Pinterest board or site, another social media website, e-mail or other sources. This is a great opportunity for businesses to leverage their contents on social media to raise awareness of their brand.

The desire for a product may also be triggered by a need to replace an underperforming item or find a solution to a problem. At this stage of the consumer's journey, a potential consumer may have recognized symptoms of a problem or challenge and may desire to find a solution to the problem. The potential consumer may search google or a social media sites for solution. Businesses will do well if they are included in the search results. They can provide contents that relates to some of the issues a consumer may face i.e. underperforming products or raising awareness of some of the symptoms and addressing them on social media to be included in search results.

Businesses or retailers will do well by engaging with their customers and potential customers to raise awareness of their products. Facebook has the greatest engagement rate (comScore, 2016) and was ranked first with 90.2 percent of global shares followed by Twitter (statista.com, 2017). Facebook and Twitter are useful social media sites for raising awareness because of their high user engagement rate and capacity to share content. Pinterest is another social media site that drives spontaneous purchasing, people look for inspiration on this site. It is good for raising awareness. Snapchat is good for attracting young people.

Businesses can also show their customers how their products can solve their problem or increase their pleasure and also how their product is better than their competitors' products. SEO and blogging is very important at this stage. Businesses can optimize their keywords on search engine so that potential clients can find them easily when looking for solutions to their problems.

Effective businesses distinguish themselves from their competitors by providing information that clarifies the consumer's pain, need, or challenge.

What action can a business take?

A business can:

- Create blogs which address some of the challenges facing potential customers. The blog/posts should focus on the business' keywords, potential challenges and should be filled with targeted keyword that will help their content to be found.

- Create shareable social media contents related to the pains, challenges, or general questions buyers are asking (FAQ). Infographics, e-books, videos, testimonials and interactive content are great assets to answer the key questions buyers have.

Awareness

Snap Election – targeting the youth

Snapchat played a key role in recent British election. Snapchat which is used by 10 million Brits every day teamed up with the electoral Commission to remind users to register. The site has a huge audience among young adults. Users posting selfies on the mobile social media platform used geofilter to show friends that they are eligible to vote in the election. Before the general election in June 2017, figures showed that 30 percent of adult under 34 are not registered to vote, compared to 4 percent adult over 55. In 2015 election only 43 percent of 18-24-year-old voted. This partnership resulted in a huge increase in the number of 18-24-year-old voting and a major increase in 18-24 year olds supporting the labor party.

Useful Statistics

% of U.S. adults who use each social media platform (2017) PEW

	Facebook	Instagram	Pinterest	LinkedIn	Twitter
Men	67%	23%	15%	28%	21%
Women	69%	32%	38%	23%	21%

Users	Facebook	Instagram	Pinterest	LinkedIn	Twitter
18-29	88%	59%	36%	34%	36%
30-49	79%	31%	32%	31%	22%
50-64	61%	13%	24%	21%	18%
65+	36%	5%	9%	11%	6%

PEW 2017

- 72 percent of online users with incomes over $75,000 use Facebook,
- 74 percent of Facebook users have some form of higher education.

JetBlue Twitter vs Facebook

JetBlue, an airline company began its social media activities with Twitter before becoming active on Facebook. Jetblue selected Twitter instead of other social media sites because Twitter was more mobile-friendly and good for raising awareness. Twitter gave JetBlue an opportunity to directly engage with users while experiencing the product. Although many JetBlue enthusiasts originally followed the company's tweets because they like the brand, JetBlue used Twitter to raise awareness of its brand and to reach those people who were not yet customers. Twitter gives the prospective audience a chance to experience JetBlue before flying with the company.

For both the loyal customers and the potential customers, Twitter is a medium for engagement and raising awareness of the products and services. Also, customers on Twitter were likely to be talking about a product while using or in the process of using the product. For example, customers travelling on the airline tweeted about the company and its products while experiencing the product at the airport i.e. check-in, you don't necessarily see that on Facebook. Furthermore, content creation was easier on Twitter than Facebook because the company could come up with content just by responding to others' comments.

Using multi-channels to raise awareness: Online and offline channels

Both online and offline channels are effective in creating consumer awareness and demand, especially when they are used together. Research by KPMG shows that social media drives roughly equal amounts of online and in-store purchasing. 52 percent of consumers cited at least one offline channel as a source of initial awareness, and 59 percent cited one or more online channels. Consumers of certain products would want to feel or see the products before buying it. For example, in the beauty and cosmetics industry most women get their beauty tips from online social media subscription channel like Ipsy and Birchbox and buy in-store where they can feel or see the product. The implication for retailers is that they can integrate online and offline channels to successful raise awareness of their products and services.

An online retailer integrate Online and offline channels

Muji, a global retail brand sells over 7, 000 household goods including furniture, clothes and food items internationally. It targets consumers based on demographics (generation X,Y), market size(leading total consumer spending in a region) and consumer behaviors (trendy group). For example, in Japan the retailer targets Generation X, because they have a high interest in shopping, and also have the disposable income. In contrast, in East Asia particularly in China, Millennials are the main target because they are very trendy and digital.

The retailer does not advertise its products the traditional way, but rather relies on consumer word of mouth. Muji has built a loyal customer base and community by providing interactive contents and engaging with its customers in product development and by asking for their ideas and opinions.

Its strategy is to communicate its concepts to consumers looking for new trends, style and information. It uses its large loyal online community, Muji.net and online loyalty program Muji passport to regularly communicate concepts, products and also provide information that can be shared on Facebook or Instagram to attract consumers to their website or stores.   The retailer uses its loyalty program to encourage customers to provide feedback and also raise awareness of its products online.

It has integrated the user's online and offline experience to market its brands.   Members receive 'MUJI Miles' for shopping with the retailer, checking into stores, posting product comments or participating in other promotions. Muji knows that in certain categories i.e. fashion products, consumers may want to see, touch or try the product to see if it fits before buying it later online. The company has made it easier for customers to go from shopping offline to online. To allow customers to then purchase the items online, they ensure that products can be easily ordered and quickly delivered.

Stage 2: Consideration

Product and company research: This is when consumers decide to research the product and company online or offline.   Once it dawns on the consumer that they have a particular problem or pain point, they begin to research solutions for their problems.   72% of buyers turn to google to research the products and companies that offer solution. The first stage of research begins with general search terms as potential buyers explore the options at their disposal. They then limit their search on specifics, focusing on specs and features and narrowing down their brand consideration set. At this stage, buyers are usually looking for information, educational material, customer reviews, and testimonials at this stage. The potential customer may research the company by reading online reviews, company website, visiting the physical shop and by speaking to friends and family about the product. Companies can make research fun and easy by integrating consumer reviews, expert opinions with enriching personal experiences on their website and social media sites.

Consumers may also turn to social media during the consideration stage of the journey. ODM Group, a digital marketing agency reports that 74% of consumers rely on social networks to guide them at this stage of their journey. A Deloitte study confirms this, and also indicates that consumers who use social media during their shopping process are 4 times more likely than non-users to spend more or significantly more on purchases as a result of a digital shopping experience.

Consumers are looking for information to make informed decisions. Historically, customers visited a store to collect any information they could about products and made their decision during that trip. The store was most likely their only source of product information. Today, as the number of information sources have increased, the digital-enabled customer can actively decide where among their many sources to look for the best information. Trust is important to them in selecting the best source. Many of them are increasingly relying on social media to make decisions on their purchases. These consumers look to influencers through social media, often friends or family, subject matter experts, or independent bloggers, for their trusted information. They also visit review sites to assess everything from quality to price to customer service, as evaluated by complete strangers. The common trend these days is that many consumers place their trust in these influencers specifically because they are not directly connected to the retailers or brands and may have experienced the product and are therefore able to give genuine feedback about the product.

This trend has impacted on the traditional role of marketing and caused retailers to lose their influence in the market place as they compete with information from different sources particularly from social media. A different perspective is required by the retailer to overcome this challenge. Instead of seeing themselves as losing control and influence, they can focus on creating and managing more authentic contents and build better relationships with influencers through their marketing campaigns to enable them to achieve a greater level of authenticity. Influencers shape consumer decision-making by advocating, promoting and popularizing the brand. It is therefore important for them to be equip with authentic information so that the retailer's voice is heard through them in the market place amidst information from different sources about their product.

Trust in online reviews over company websites have also created a risk for many companies, since they lack control over messaging and product information contained in consumer reviews. Companies can overcome this challenge by creating or providing quality products and services, informative websites, good customer services, engage and involve their customers in the creation of products to ensure that they gain favorable reviews on social media and other online review sites.

Consumers are also looking for personalization of services. Companies may use permissioned data to personalize the products and services they offer their customers. They can leverage consumer data to provide effective personalization for their customers. Analyzing consumer data can give them better insight and understanding of consumer behavior to enable them to personalize their products and services. For example, using insight gained from analyzing data, companies can offer individual deals, coupons, or recommendations and promotion to the consumer based on previous purchase and or behavior.

Key influencers at the consideration stage include price, brand reputation, promotion, deals, product feature, samples, peer influences/recommendations, price comparison sites, word-of-mouth, brand and or product sites, and online reviews. Product decision factors varies by category. For example, for fashion and luxury items, brand reputation is an important consideration factor, although price is still the top decision factor. For electronics, product features are most important, followed by price, brand reputation and online reviews.

Example of personalization

An excellent example of personalization is how Sony used Twitter to increase sales. By providing its 1,500 twitter users an opportunity to personalize their Vaio laptop, Sony was able to successfully increase sales of Vaio laptop by $1.5 million.

Stage 3: Conversion

Deciding where and when to buy

At this stage of the consumer's journey, the consumer decides where, and when to buy a product. Key influencers at this stage include price, product features and website. Price and product features are the most important factor in choosing where to buy especially in categories like electronics. Equally important is a trusted website, although this may vary across different age groups. For example, Millennials are comparatively more likely than the older generations to choose a brand or company based on price than website because of their low income and ease with online shopping.

Social media is another tool that drives people to buy. Research from America and the UK shows that social media influence purchases online and offline. Some customers browse online and buy offline. 4 in 10 social media users have purchased an item online or in-store after sharing or favoriting it on Twitter, Facebook or Pinterest. Half of the purchasing takes place within 1 week of sharing or favoriting the item on social media. Pinterest is the site most likely to drive spontaneous purchasing. Factors such as providing users with additional product information, where to buy the product, offers and coupon code, reviews and recommendation and pricing information may contribute to the quick drive towards purchase. Each network drives purchasing for a different reasons, so it is important for companies to find the network that works for their products.

Other factors that influence where a consumer decides to buy include online review, brand reputation, delivery options and price, stock availability, peer advice and returns policy. For example, consumers buying fashion items are most likely to choose a company based on brand reputation, availability of stock and also on returns policy.

The implication for retailers is to consider these factors influencing the consumer's decision to buy at this stage and offer some solutions. For example, an electronics retailers provide competitive prices and information on product features and how it can benefit the consumer.

Stage 4: Evaluation

Experience and feedback

This is the final stage of the consumer's journey. At this stage, the consumer has used the product at home, the next thing the consumer may do is to try to validate their choice by comparing their own experience with the product with what others are saying about the products.

Depending on the type of product, consumers may have to assemble the product by following instructions i.e. a new electronic product before using it. They may experience difficulties if the instructions are not clear or complicated. Companies can provide how-to tips and set-up help with videos on YouTube or provide experts help on Skype. Companies can also personalize the at-home experience by creating incentives to share their experience.

Consumers may share their experience on social media by posting, joining or following brand on social media, or through conventional word of mouth i.e. share their opinions with friends, family or review the product online. Key influencers include product performance. Positive customer experiences can significantly influence future buying decisions positively, and a negative experience may have a negative impact. A positive customer experience can generate loyalty and repeat purchase and a negative customer experience may affect sales negatively and impact on profit.

It also important that companies understand where consumers are posting feedback so that they can monitor and nurture positive online customer reviews. Recent trends indicate that consumers are increasingly using social media to provide feedback. They are using social media sites such as Facebook, Twitter, WhatsApp, Instagram and blogs for posting and reviewing feedback. The implication for companies is that user-generated reviews are being posted on sites that are increasingly beyond their control or influence. Companies can overcome some of these challenges by integrating social media into their marketing strategies. Many popular online retailers have feedback mechanisms built in to solicit comments from customers shortly after their customers receive their goods. Additionally, companies can proactively reach out to satisfied customers and encourage them to post reviews. For example, they can provide consumers incentives to share their experience with the company.

To understand how social media is driving consumers from social media to purchase, business may have to combine social media data, transaction data and consumer survey.

You can survey or ask your customers questions to determine their:

Demographics

- Find out your customer's demographics: age, gender, education and household income. The answers will enable you to determine the websites you can easily locate them i.e. more women use Pinterest. You can also use the answers to figure out your target audience.

Identify the social networks your customers use and how often they use them.

- Find out which networks and sites your customers post their contents to, and how often?
- Find out if they have ever purchased an item in the store or online after they shared or tweeted the item.
- Identifying the most effective social media to reach each segment of your customers.

Identify their interest in each network – to enable you to provide suitable contents that meet their interest and needs

- Find out their topic of interest, what photos, videos or stories they are interested in on each social media site?
- Which product category do they often shop for?

Determine their behavior online

- Find out whether they have purchased an item either in-store or online after they have tweeted / retweeted / or favorited it on social media? Where did they buy the item i.e. online or in store?
- Have they bought any of your products after sharing or tweeting or favoriting it on social media?
- If so, which item and from which category? Which network did they find the item or shared it on?
- Find out if they have purchased an item they have seen on social media they have not shared or favourite? Which network did they find that item? Why they bought this item?
- Find out if they have purchased any of your competitors' products after seeing or sharing them on a social network? Find out the social media networks and how often this has happen.

Overall, these questions will enable you to determine which social networks drive the most sales and then you can allocate your resources effectively depending on your goals. You can also use your insight to provide contents that will meet your customers' interest.

Identify the network that works for your product

- Find out what your customers like about each network i.e. which network is easy to use, provides inspiration, remind me when a sale is taking place.
- What they dislike about each network?
- Which network influenced their decision to purchase?
- Find out how favoriting, pinning any of your items influence their decision to buy.
- Find out what else might have influenced their decision to buy on each network i.e. additional information, reviews and recommendations.
- What kind of information influenced their decision?
- Find out what is most important in influencing their decision to buy i.e. recommendation from friends and families, independent reviews or promotional code.

Generally, this would determine which social networks is right for your products and also enable you to provide the right contents and deals for each network to meet your customers' needs.

Pricing

- How did the price of the item influence your customers' decision?
- Find out if your customers are influenced by quality rather than price.
- Did comparative tools i.e. price comparative tool influenced their decision to purchase?

Mobile Shopping

- Find out if your customers use their mobiles for shopping.
- What activities do they use them for i.e. making purchase, researching a product, finding information about physical location of the retailer?
- Find out what they use it for i.e. comparing prices, using promotional code.
- Find out how they access your website. Find out which apps they use for shopping.
- Find out if they have shared content about your brand or product on their mobile phone.
- Find out the category of products they have shared.
- Find out the content? How did they share it i.e. on social media? Their challenges in using mobile phones in shopping?

Generally, these information would enable you to create the right contents and offers for mobile customers.

Timeline: from Sharing to buying

- Find out how long it takes your customers from sharing to buying the product i.e. instantly, one week, a month etc.
- Find out which networks move your customers to purchase more quickly i.e. do customers who share your content on Pinterest move quickly to purchase?
- Find out what would enable them to respond spontaneously.
- Find out how each segment of your customers move quickest from sharing to purchasing.

These questions will help you to understand the duration of your customers' interest, enable you to offer deals and incentives with the right deadlines and to target your social media promotions when sharers are most likely to buy

CHAPTER 11

The Future of The Social Technologies And Its Impact On Our Lives

The last few years have seen major changes in the way we communicate, collaborate, consume and share information due to social technologies. Social technologies have impacted our behavior and all aspects of our lives from health, education, politics, business and our social lives, although it carries some risks. For example, billions of people have adopted new behaviors using social media. From keeping up with friends, getting news update, sharing personal events to organizing support for political and social causes.

Although we have seen major changes, the impact of social technologies on our lives and business remain embryonic today, but it could ultimately surpass our imaginations. It is beginning to deliver its potential value and more of this value will be realized in the coming years as technology advances and more people have access to the internet and join social platforms. Without any doubt, the impact of social technology will be felt cross various sectors of the economy and our social lives and may offer solution to many challenging problems facing societies across the world.

Health

Social technology will have a profound impact on health care, for example, improving healthcare. More community healthcare platforms such as QuestionDoctors.com and CrowdMed, will give physicians opportunities to provide quick and convenient care for free or at a low cost enabling physicians to serve their patients better. QuestionDoctors.com allows users globally to ask questions directly to a board certified medical doctors and consultants on its crowdsourcing platform. Users are offered free medical help or in some cases are encouraged to pay a token. Communities like FSermo, and Wego also provide forums for discussing treatment. Users can discuss concerns, share their experiences, seek advice, and overcome the stigma that too often is associated with chronic disease.

There will be more applications of social technologies to help improve individual health. The community and communication elements of social technology will enable the formation of more patient-focused networks, often built around a particular health condition or disease to significantly improve and help individuals manage their health. For example, social health platforms such as PatientsLikeMe.com, HealthCrowd, and HealthUnlocked provide supportive environment for patients to connect and pool their knowledge, share their experiences, and help reinforce beneficial behavior. Individuals and their families also receive support, insights and potential leads on new treatments and innovative tools for their conditions.

Some examples of social communities

ConnectedLiving: is a community of seniors, a rapidly growing population of users. Currently available through nursing homes, assisted living complexes, and other senior housing centers.

Doctors.net.uk: doctors' forum for discussing clinical issues. Thousands of doctors use this forum each day for clinical questions and general discussion on health.

Sermo: provides forums in which physicians can discuss treatment options.

PatientsLikeMe.com: is a patient community where patients with particular health conditions can pool their knowledge, share their experiences and support each other.

HealthUnlocked : is a social networking platform that uses AI (artificial intelligence) to support patients to better manage their own health by recommending relevant content, information and services to patients customized to their needs.

Future applications of social technology will also be seen in the use of social tools to address global health challenges such as educating patients about diseases. For example, as more nations and health organizations shift their health-care strategy from one based on treatment of disease to one focused on prevention and wellness, social tools could be used to educate people and raise awareness of health issues and diseases. An example of this application, is the use of social tools with virtual reality and Gaming Environments to educate patients on the prevention of diseases i.e. Multi-User Virtual Environments (MUVEs), a three-dimensional environment, which allows users to interact with each other through a virtual representation of themselves (known as an avatar).

Social tools will also enable clinicians and medical experts across the globe to collaborate and work together to offer advice and effective treatment for patients in a virtual world i.e. virtualsimcenter.clinispace.com. Additionally, Social tools will enable health care services to target the right audience for their training programs. Physicians will also be able to use social tools like Twitter, YouTube to promote patient health care education. They can tweet, create blogs, record videos, and participate in disease-specific discussion forums focused on patient education.

Applications for preventive health and "keeping people well" (i.e. Good Samaritan's LivingWell@Home application) will grow as healthcare shift to preventive and patient-focus treatment. Again, the ability to quickly disseminate information and mobilize large numbers of people will make social media a powerful tool to facilitate greater progress towards public health goals i.e. public education advocacy regarding public health issues.

There will be more opportunities to leverage social tools with mobile, analytics and cloud to transform health research i.e. clinical trials. CliniOps, a California company leverages social tools, mobile, analytics and cloud to address the challenge of manual traditional clinical trials which is time-consuming. The company is also using these technology to address the challenge of gathering information in emerging markets that lack broadband Internet access, widespread computer literacy, and knowledge. Wego is another company that uses AI system to monitor user's content to select volunteers for clinical trials. There will be more applications similar to these examples.

Another health challenge that social tools will be useful in addressing is adherence and ultimately health care outcomes. Adherence is a big issue. One of the most common reasons patients return to the hospital or suffer medical setbacks is lack of adherence to their medication plan. The issue of adherence causes healthcare institutions billions of money and prevents better outcome to treatment. Social features such as community and communication will facilitate the formation of supportive groups which will enable patients to engage in the treatment prescribed. For example, members of a group can discuss issues, share their experiences, provide support for each other and encourage adherence to drug and healthcare routine. Additionally, issues such as the impact of drugs and treatment i.e. side effects of drugs could be detected early as patients share their experiences with others in the community and health providers who are engaged and listening on social platforms can detect the problem early and offer solution to address the problem.

The communication and collaboration that social tools enable in enterprises could also be applied to health, enabling professionals to work together across geographical boundaries to research health issues, share ideas and research outcomes and solve problems together. There will be more partnership and collaboration between patients, health care organizations, medical experts, medical equipment and products manufacturers to improve the efficiency and performance of health organizations. For example, patients groups could collaborate with pharmaceuticals companies in the development of life changing medicines. Additionally, there will be the creation of more supportive platform that would enable patients to share their experiences with others and genuinely connect and gain support from people going through the same thing creating value for them. Patients could also benefit from improvements in diagnostics, devices, services and the creation of drugs and products which better meets their needs from their shared experiences and feedbacks. Manufacturers and companies could use their feedback and data to personalized medicine for patients. There are huge opportunities for companies to analyze the data to determine how patients respond to treatment, the types of patients who will respond well to which types of treatment and the possibility to customize treatment plans and better selection of patients for clinical trials with higher rate of success. Furthermore, collaboration between health providers, manufacturers of medical products, and other stakeholders will help to improve operational efficiency, reduce cost and ultimately improve the performance of health care organizations.

The role of influencers will increase as more people and more people continue to use social tools like blog, Twitter, Snapchat, Instagram and YouTube to share their experiences of living with their illness. Patients with large followers will be able to reach out to large audiences to influence them. They will also be able to provide information, insights and advocate for communities that too often feel they have no voice i.e. #hospitalglam. Barby Ingle, the founder of #hospitalglam has more than 26,000 Twitter followers, who seek her guidance in dealing with health insurance and living with chronic pain. There is also a growing number of companies hiring these patient influencers to reach out and understand their community and ultimately to sell them products that meet their needs. Influencers will be able to provide feedback from their community and also work together with pharmaceutical firms, medical device manufacturers, hospitals, and insurers to design products that meet their community needs.

Finally, all the stages of the patient's journey will be affected by big data beginning from first contact with the service to medical research. Social health data will allow doctors and health professionals to build better health profiles and predictive models to more effectively anticipate, diagnose and treat diseases. By leveraging big data and scientific advancements, researchers and health organization will be able to build a health system that goes beyond curing disease to preventing disease. Global Public Health Intelligence Network (www.who.int/en) is an example of a medical crowd sourcing initiative set up by the Canadian government and the World Health Organization to monitor online news reports. Data from this platform is used effectively by the government to monitor and spot any trends in infectious diseases to keep the public safe from outbreak such as Severe Acute Respiratory Syndrome. Healthmap (healthmap.org) is another medical crowdsourcing platform that can be used by individuals and medical professionals in real time to alert the public about diseases so that such areas could be avoided and diseases contained.

Education

More of the value potential of social tools will be realized in applying social tools to improve educational effectiveness in future. For example, some of the limitation due to distance and time in educational service delivery will be overcome in the coming years using social tools. There will be more application of Web 2.0 technology to support student collaboration and research. Microblogging tools such as Twitter, Vodcasting, Slideshares and YouTube to support learning or as a do-it-yourself tool for reinforce lessons.

Social tools could be integrated with VR (Virtual Reality) to improve education. VR can improve engagement, constructivist learning, and creativity and provide an opportunity for students to virtually experience abstract concepts. Features of Virtual reality such as interactivity, intuitive, fun, hands-on and immersive experience provides an innovative and a fresh way of learning for students. For example, Google Expeditions tool is fun and allows students to take virtual field trips to Mars, Amazon Rain Forest and historic sites such as the Great Walls of China and pyramid of Egypt, which can trigger new interest in the subject, provide a shared experience for better classroom discussion, and improve overall engagement.

Research has shown VR improves students' learning outcome and students are able to use their virtual experiences to build their own understanding of their own world and also apply the knowledge gained to solve real world problems. It is a great learning tool as it gives students the opportunity to experience the activities they are studying. For example, it can be used as a virtual learning environment for law students to learn how to manage a "real" legal case.

It is anticipated that merging the immersive characteristics of the VR with social technologies will improve collaboration and creativity amongst students and enable them to develop self-learning skills, improve students' engagement, and transform future learning styles by facilitating the formation of learning communities, discussions and the application of technology to solve real world problems.

Furthermore, the integration of social media with virtual reality could also be used to overcome the challenge of distance and time and ultimately help to improve distance learning. With more VR platforms like AltspaceVR, WebVR, AFrame, The Verge, and LectureVR emerging, more opportunities will be available for teachers, lecturers, facilitators and students to use the combination of these technology to reach out to a large number of people in real time, enabling educational institutions to overcome the limitation of distance and time. For example, a lecturer or teacher could teach a virtual class in real time with students from all over the world. A tour facilitator will be able to guide a large group of tourist around a cultural site.

Effective learning in our modern digital world entails collaboration amongst learners, hands-on, reflection and interaction with the learning environment. The communication and collaboration feature of social tools enabled in enterprise could allow students to interact, collaborate on tasks, and solve problems together across the world in real time irrespective of geographical location. Examples include students collaborating across the world on science projects, educational institutions collaborating with other institutions on projects and research staff collaborating to write a research article. Also, sharing, gaming and participation enabled by social technology could unleashed creativity in large numbers of people enabling them to work together to solve very challenging problems.

Crowd sourcing is another area where social tools could be used to address educational challenges. Crowd sourcing could generate ideas from large number of people to solve problems. In educational setting, it could be used as an innovation lab where solutions to case studies could be crowdsourced or as a resource for tapping into the collective wisdom of the educational community.

Research

There will be more integration of social tools with scientific research to improve scalability. Many diseases in the world have several strains and manifest themselves in different forms in different part of the world. The challenge is in detecting the different strains, which involves testing billions of people every year and working with researchers, health workers, pharmaceutical companies and medical professionals across the world to diagnose and find cure for the diseases.

The community feature of social tools will enable researchers over the world to communicate and share their discoveries (i.e. the unique strain in their country) in real time to improve diagnosis of disease. An example of this, is the integration of the community feature of social tools with the Prakash foldscope to explore microscopic environments in different parts of the world. Users across the world share images of their discoveries with peers, researchers and other stakeholders which could accelerate research, diagnosis and cure for the malaria disease.

The Prakash lab plans to release a one dollar folding paper microscope, called the Foldscope, to more than million people in 135 countries for research and education (2017). The cheap, pocket-size microscope can achieve magnification above 2,000 times using standard laboratory slide samples and is powerful enough to detect malaria parasite in a drop of blood and is accessible to everyone. For malaria, imaging is important in research and diagnosing the disease. The foldscope will enable more users including school children, laboratory technicians and the world's best scientists around the world to share powerful images of the different strains of the mosquito parasite with researchers leading to less waiting time for diagnosis, cure and potential breakthrough in eradicating the disease. The foldscope community will also be able to discuss the parasite, cure and new discoveries, insight and medication for the disease.

Business

Technological advancement has changed the way we fundamentally consume goods and services. Consumers now live in a world connected by smart phones, GPS and social media and expect businesses to deliver personalize experiences to them on their devices anytime anywhere. To succeed in this new world, businesses need to shift from the traditional way of designing and manufacturing products based on anticipating user's needs and rather start with the end-users in order to deliver personalize service to them. To know what the consumer wants, businesses will need to know and understand their consumers. They need to know who they are, what they do, what drives them, how they feel, their likes and dislikes and their hobbies, etc. Social technology can play a crucial role in determining who the end-users are, through their profile, the exact needs of the user, how they feel, their interest and hobbies.

In future, we will see more application of social media to address the challenge of the paradigm shift from traditional way of building products to one that start with the user, engages with the user to determine their needs and co-create products with them. Collaboration enabled by enterprise social tools will enable cross functional internal teams to collaborate and build products using feedback, insight and recommendation from social media users and other consumers' data in order to personalize services to them. This approach creates more value and is efficient.

We will see wider applications of social media and artificial intelligence in manufacturing similar to brewing beer with AI. IntelligentX Brewing in UK, used AI to create the first artificial intelligence beer. The company, IntelligentX Brewing, a joint venture between creative agency 10X and machine learning specialist Intelligent Layer used real time customer feedback interpreted using machine learning algorithm to change four of its products Golden AI, Amber AI, Pale AI and Black AI. Codes on the bottles direct customers to a Facebook Messenger bot for feedback, which is interpreted by the algorithm and used to tweak the recipes for the beer.

Seeing the power of social media applications at the consumer level, many marketers will embrace the ability of these tools to spread their messages. Trends such as availability of data, affordability of computers and deep learning systems will enable big organizations to target consumers with the right messages that are relevant to their interest to boost their engagement and ultimately increase their revenue. Our smart phones generates massive data about our location, who we are communicating with, our web browsing history and with sensors can generate our health data. Social media also generates information about our demographics, our likes, dislikes, friends and interest. Combing data from our social media, our smart phone, data generated from organizations (i.e. supermarket or credit card) with AI, organizations will be able to target users with the right messages relevant to them, customize the message to their interest in order to optimize their experience. In the process they will increase their revenue.

For example, Google, Amazon and Facebook use AI to suggest content to users. Facebook suggests content, friends and relevant articles and adverts to users using their data and AI to optimize their user experience and also maximize their revenue.

The impact of social technologies is expected to grow in business, as productivity improves due to the application of social tools. Social technologies, have the potential to unlock the initiative, creativity, and passion that are necessary to produce innovations and to enable companies to address the most difficult problems. The interactions, relationship and collaboration enabled by social technologies can encourage more engaged employees to be innovative and creative. Furthermore, fully networked organizations (networked internally and externally) will have the opportunity to improve productivity and consequently their market share due to better relationship with customers, involving customers in product development and collaboration among staff and other stakeholders. Employees will be able to share good practice and quickly work together to resolve issues.

Recruitment

As the world become more globalized and connected, social technologies will be used to address the challenge of talent management. Social tools can be used at all the different stages of talent management (identification, recruitment, development, deployment and retention) to reduce cost, improve recruiters' efficiency and help to find the right talent for business success.

Finding and recruiting quality talent has never been more critical. In a global world, organizations face challenges such as competition, economic uncertainty, and high costs making it difficult to thrive and make profit. These challenges has increased the pressure to find the right people for the success of the business. It is estimated that recruiting a top performer has the potential to increase a company's revenue by 10 – 100 times each year. Also, in some organizations the tenure of senior staff and CEO is about two and half years and it may take about 6 - 9 months to recruit, which is not cost effective considering how much time and money is spent during the search and the recruitment process. Good talent management is therefore becoming increasingly urgent and important in a global world and for the success of an organization. Social media can be used to address this problem by enabling recruiters to advertise and match people with the right skills in a short time.

Secondly, it is estimated that worldwide, organizations spend more than $85 billion each year to source candidates. Much of the money for acquiring talent is spent on sourcing, including recruiting agency fees and recruitment advertising costs for new hires. Social tools can improve sourcing of talent, reduce cost drastically by eliminating agency and adverts fees and can also help to attract and identify the right candidates for the job. For example, a company can advertise a job on social media at relatively low cost instead of through normal media and agency; use candidates profile and social maps to identify the right candidate. Social tools can be used to screen large numbers of profiles and to identify people with specific expertise. Using the candidate's profile will enable recruiters to narrow down suitable candidates and also help them to assess candidate's skills, experience, history and interest at a shorter time compared to the traditional long time for screening applications. Additionally, social networking sites provides crucial profiling information i.e. demographic and behavior data (sharing interest in environmental and liking of human rights group), which are difficult to obtain through traditional method. Recruiters can also validate candidates through existing connections and references. Considerable time is saved by narrowing down candidates considering over 100 applications are received for every job vacancy and it is estimated that about 60% of all candidates that apply are unqualified.

Furthermore, social tools can help to improve the matching of people to positions, help recruiters to recruit faster from a wider network of qualified candidates i.e. LinkedIn and Xing. Effective matching of candidates will speed the recruitment process by enabling HR departments to quickly make recruitment decisions and also help identify the most-qualified employee. Also, issues such as mismatch on local, national and global market can be eliminated by transparency into supply and demand due to social technology.

Additionally, communication, building and maintaining better relationship with candidates play a critical role in identifying, developing, and sustaining long-term relationships with candidates and existing employees. Social tools can improve the experience of active and passive job seekers by building stronger relationships with them. Employers can communicate directly with potential candidates during the recruitment process and better engage with them using social tools. They can communicate with them from the time they submit their application, acknowledging application, share information about their company, and provide a status update of the job using social tools.

Social tools can also be used for post-recruitment tasks such as allocating tasks, selecting project teams and training staff. Organizations can provide new staff a social graph of relevant staffs and experts who can help them settle in quickly. Top performers and experts can share their knowledge and experience with new recruits directly or through forums.

Finally, the ability to recruit the right person for the job enabled by social technology could lead to higher productivity and consequently better work satisfaction and ultimately higher retention rates.

Social problems

There will be more opportunities to use social tool to address social problem such as isolation. One of the greatest risks of aging is losing our social networks. The loss of friends, peer connection, coupled with increasing limited physical mobility, can lead to isolation. Companies such as Facebook, SeniorMaze, MyBoomerplace, coolgrandma, efamily, Tapestry, Stitch and Honor are using social tools to connect and provide services online to overcome this problem. Platforms like Facebook and SeniorMaze offer a platform for seniors to connect with their peers, keeping them engage and making them feel less isolation. Honor also connects homecare professionals with clients based on their individual needs. For example, it can connecting seniors who need help with housework or a ride to a doctor to users who can provide that help. The app also enables family members to monitor the service.

Additionally, technologies such as sensors, GPS, and senior-focused social networks can help seniors continue to live at home. Qualcomm is an example of a company that is focused on leveraging existing cloud technology to create digital platforms that connect medical devices to remote monitoring systems. Qualcomm Life's 2net™ captures the biometric data collected from wearables and integrates it with other health-related data to deliver better health care remotely. The platform brings together care teams and patients to better manage patients' illness and improve their quality of life.

Social problems like crime and poverty can also be addressed with social media. More crimes have been solved using social media to identify criminals and their activities. Connectivity, interactivity and scale has enabled organizations to quickly identify criminals by circulation incidents on social media. Through sharing the message is able to reach a wide audience and the criminals identified. Poverty is another challenge that social tools can help to address. Social platform could be used to tap into community networks to tackle issues of poverty such as childcare for low income families. There will be development of care application that taps into the trust and community features of social tools. CareSwap is an example of a social platform that uses the web and mobile app to help low-income families address the issue of childcare within their trusted networks of friends, neighbours and family. Flexible, affordable childcare provision is essential in supporting parents to improve their income through work or by accessing education and training, which ultimately helps to reduce poverty.

The social sector contribution to addressing social challenges will be enhanced with social tools. Social tools can help connect organizations with volunteers and donors. Geographical constraints which limits fund raising and recruitment of volunteers could be address using social tools. Volunteers across the world will be able to connect to causes instantly through social media. Donors irrespective of their location could donate to causes anywhere at any time. Non-profit organizations and other social sector organizations could also use social technologies to raise funds, collect and analyze information, recruit and expand their volunteer networks, crowdsource solutions, raise awareness, educate the public and boost engagement using social tools. During natural disaster, social tools could help victims and volunteers send information about their location and the help they need to social platforms.

In future, it is the relationships that businesses develop with their stakeholders i.e. customers that will help them create value. For most organizations to realize the full potential of social technologies, there must be changes in organizational structure, processes and culture that strengthen relationships. For example, a structural change from a hierarchical to flatter organizational structure will strengthen relationship between employees and encourage them to share knowledge regardless of position, title, role or department leading to increase organizational knowledge, openness and transparency. A change in culture to that of sharing will empower employees at all levels with knowledge to make decision quickly to resolve issues.

Better relationship and trust is also required for successful collaborative work and engaging with customers. Change does not happen overnight, it is ongoing. It will therefore take time to achieve the changes that is necessary to reap the full value of social technologies.

CHAPTER 12

Source of Value of Social Technologies

Today we are more connected than any generation before us. The connections we have made through social media has enabled us to build better relationship with people and businesses around the world, which is necessary for today's dynamic and globalize world.

Features of social technology such as its ability to expand interaction in terms of speed, scale and its ability to record interaction has enabled it to create value. For example, at the click of a button, a user can communicate instantly with a large audience at no cost. Additionally, communication and collaborative features of social tools can improve productivity. The ability to record interaction can enlighten businesses about consumer conversations, influence and also create social connections which can be analysed and used to improve business performance and efficiency. For example, insight gained from consumer conversations can be used to improve production and operational performance. Insight can be derived from social connection to determine influencers, who can be used as advocate for a brand.

The participative feature of social media is also a source of value as it enables discussions and the opportunity for people to discuss and share their opinions about products and services. Insight gained from tapping into the discussions and opinions of the crowd can be used to understand industry dynamics i.e. analysing real-time responses to changes in the industry (TweetReach is a useful tool). By also, listening and analysing sentiments and emotions from i.e. Facebook followers and fans and from other social media platforms, firms can gain new insights and innovations about future trends. They can also determine opportunities in the market by using analytic tools (text analytic tools) to determine the market size. For example, analysing direct feedback from the crowd will determine whether consumers like a product or not and consequently the opportunities and market size of a product. Firms can gain consumer insights by analysing consumer sentiments to determine consumers' reaction to a product. Analytic tool like Social Mention is useful in analysing consumer insights.

In terms of collaboration, employees and teams can collaborate internally and externally (customers) to create value by collaborating to build better products using enterprise social technology. The benefits of using collaborative Web 2.0 technologies, which enables firms to connect employees internally and extend the organization's reach to customers, agencies, suppliers and other partners will also enable organizations to gain competitive advantage from greater efficiency, low production cost, improved performance, lower prices, quality and may result in increased market share and more profits. Furthermore, collaboration can provide value by helping businesses to provide responsive service i.e. network intelligence collected from collaborating with customers, manufacturers, suppliers, shippers, delivery companies, industry experts could be used to provide responsive service to customers i.e. response to changes.

The community feature of social technology can be utilized by businesses to create value by encouraging customers to solve each other's problem. Customers can gain value from getting instant solutions at any time to their problems from other customers who have experienced the product and also get more value out of their products and services. It is a win-win situation for the customer and the business as customer service cost is reduced.

Social tools have enabled individuals to connect and form communities with other individuals around the world for fun and in crisis. Like organizations, it has enabled them to gain more insight, use their collective intelligence and influence to solve problems and impact the world around them. Individuals can benefit from lower prices and better products which meet their needs because of transparency, insight and co-creation with businesses.

It has given businesses the opportunity to build better relationship with their stakeholders and empowered employees for success. Employees can engage, collaborate and share information with other employees and customers around the world. The relationships developed through collaboration will enable employees to build trust, which is necessary for sharing information and working together in teams to achieve business goals.

Businesses can benefit from increased sales revenues as a result of increase customer acquisition and increase customer retention by monitoring customer sentiment and engagement using social tools. Insight gained through feedback can be used for quicker decision-making, improve strategy and to create better products. Businesses can save money by advertising on social media and also generate leads at low cost. They can also improve efficiency and performance because of low operational cost and improved processes.

Social technology is here to stay. Although it cannot replace face-to-face interaction, its adoption is on the rise. Around 1 in every 3 minutes spent online is dedicated to social networking and messaging and the number of worldwide users is expected to reach about 2.95 billion by 2020, around a third of the Earth's entire population (www.statista.com). There are more than 50 million small businesses using Facebook Pages to connect with their customers.

A social media presence is not enough to generate value from social media. Having a purposeful social media strategy which aligns with the business goal will ensure success. Also, taking advantage of social media features like speed, scale, interaction, communication, collaboration to build better relationship through sharing, capturing knowledge, utilizing collective intelligence, empowering employees to take action will ensure success. For example, sales employees can interact with customers instantly, create value through better relationship with customers and peers, and gain product knowledge through sharing and access to internal captured knowledge. Sharing contents that will benefit consumers will help to build better relationships with consumers. For example, a how-to video, tips, links to free or discount coupons on subject matter or information that can address a user's problem. Furthermore, access to experts and product knowledge will enable employees to engage well with customers and equip them with the skills and knowledge to answer any query a customer may have and also drive business growth.

Despites the benefits and opportunities that social technologies provide, they also carry risks such as data protection and privacy issues. However, despite the risks, it is anticipated that the benefits of social technologies will ultimately outweigh the risks for most businesses. Technological advancement, policies and cultural change will in future help to minimize the risks.

ABOUT THE AUTHOR

S. Darling has an MSc in Business Information Systems, experience in managing data and providing management information systems.

www.ingramcontent.com/pod-product-compliance
Lightning Source LLC
Chambersburg PA
CBHW080419060326
40689CB00019B/4297